P9-DMF-899

STORM
over the
ARAB WORLD

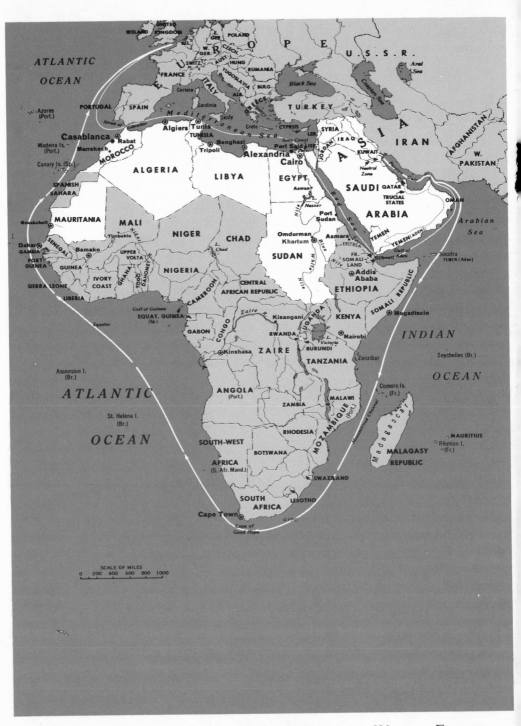

The Arab World, Africa, and Trade Routes to Western Europe

STORM
over the
ARAB
WORLD

A People in Revolution

EUGENE M. FISHER

AND

M. CHERIF BASSIOUNI

with a foreword by
Arnold Toynbee

Follett Publishing Company · Chicago

Text copyright © 1972 by Eugene Fisher and M. Cherif Bassiouni.
Maps copyright © 1972 by Follett Publishing Company, a division
of Follett Corporation. All rights reserved. No part of this
publication may be reproduced, stored in a retrieval system, or
transmitted in any form or by any means, electronic, mechanical,
photocopying, recording, or otherwise, without the prior
permission of the publisher.

Library of Congress catalog card number: 70–183181
ISBN   0–695–80037–x

Manufactured in the United States of America

DS 8
62.5
.F5

4-06-76 #4

To
RUTH
and
ROSSANNA

145358

WITHDRAWN
EMORY & HENRY LIBRARY

CONTENTS

FOREWORD

THE TITLE of this book has been well chosen. It fits the authors' subject and their particular approach to it. A storm is a temporary ordeal. It is fraught with danger so long as it lasts, and, at any moment before it is over, it may precipitate a catastrophe, but alternatively it may gradually subside without having worked irremediable havoc. Until the storm has passed, its eventual effect remains an open question. The answer mainly depends on how the people overtaken by the storm decide to react to it.

In this book, Bassiouni and Fisher have made a comprehensive survey of the Arab world since World War I. They put this stormy half-century in perspective by presenting it as one among a number of chapters of the Arabs' long history and show that Arab history is still in the making, with important further chapters still to come. "The Arab Revolution"—a term that repeatedly recurs—gives the keynote of the book. The Arab world is vast. It extends, east and west, from the east coast of Arabia to the west coast of north Africa. The many Arab communities that live within these wide bounds are still far from being homogeneous either socially or economically or politically. But, besides having inherited a common language, they are now going through a common experience. They are all passing through the same revolution, though different Arab communities are at present at different stages of it.

This current revolution is not confined to the Arab World. It is a global revolution, and its ultimate cause is the radical transformation of technology within the last two centuries. The revolution has now engulfed the western peoples who originally set it going. The Ashkenazim, who have been the ruling element in the first chapter of the history of present-day Israel, are western settlers in the Arab World, as the authors point out. A British observer can see their psychological affinity with the Protestant British and Dutch settlers in northern Ireland and in southern Africa. One of the most interesting passages in the book is the account of the domestic stresses and strains, within the Israeli community, between the Ashkenazi ex-Yiddish-speaking Israelis from Eastern Europe and the Sephardi ex-Arabic-speaking Israelis from the Arab World. The global revolution which is sweeping over the Arab countries is at work in Israel too. If Israel had been exempt from this world-wide experience, that would indeed have been surprising.

However, the subject of the book is the Arab World itself, not the Arab-Israeli conflict. Inevitably this conflict looms large in the history of the last half-century, but Bassiouni and Fisher are not obsessed by it. They see beyond it, and they reckon with the possibility that it may have an unsensational ending. While facing the alternative possibility of a tragic dénouement, they see some hope that Israel may eventually become peacefully assimilated to the Arab world into which it has injected itself, and from which more than half of the Jewish part of its population has been drawn, not to speak of the non-Jewish Palestinian Arabs within Israel's boundaries and in the further territories occupied by the Israelis since 1967. Bassiouni and Fisher are stalwart champions of the Arab cause, but they take long views: they are healthily historical-minded.

Seeing Arab history in perspective, as they do see it, they are able to be frank about the Arabs' weaknesses, besides being proud of their past and hopeful about their prospects. They of sharp dispute. Both sides of that issue will be examined in the next chapter.

The Arab People   The conflict over Palestine brought into new prominence the existence of another ethnic entity, the Arab people, embracing all those of Arabic culture throughout north Africa and southwest Asia. This ethnic-cultural group was the basis of the Arab empire which once ruled all these areas and much of the then known world. It is part of the foundation of a new Arab nationalism which today stands in armed opposition to Zionism.

The claim of Arab nationhood will be examined in a later chapter. At this point let it suffice to say that the idea of an Arab nationhood is based upon broad ethnic kinship and common cultural heritage. It embraces Muslims, Christians, Jews, and other religious communities. The claim of Jewish peoplehood rests substantially upon adherence to a political dogma based only in part on religious affiliation. Jewish peoplehood is religious in origin and almost wholly political in application.

Zionism in the United States[1]   As early as 1922 the U.S. Congress voted a joint resolution advocating a sovereign Jewish commonwealth and the United States by special treaty recognized the British mandate over Palestine with its provisions for a "national home" for the "Jewish people."

During World War II Hitler treated all Jews as part of an identifiable ethnic unit and attempted a "final settlement" of what he called "the Jewish question." Universal sympathy for the terrible suffering of European Jews created a climate in which the peoples of the west, especially in the United States, were easily persuaded that Jewishness was in fact a sign of nationhood and that the Zionist claim to Palestine as a national homeland was plausible.

Western Christians tended to see the creation of a Jewish state as atonement for the wrongs suffered by European Jews through five centuries. Support of political Zionism was in fact an attempt to salve the western conscience at no cost to the west.

That this claim to Palestine could be enforced only by replacing the Arabs of Palestine with settlers from Europe got no consideration. When Palestine was first opened to Jewish immigration, British foreign secretary Balfour insisted that the "wishes and prejudices" of indigenous Palestinians would not and need not be consulted.

No Zionist spokesman ever bothered to point out that wrongs had been inflicted upon Jews in Europe not by Arabs but by European Christians. At no place in the Arab world had Jews suffered as they had in Europe and, less extensively, in the Americas. For thirteen hundred years Arabs had welcomed Jews, treated them as equals, and lived with them in easy harmony but were now to pay the westerners' debt with their land, their property, their homes, and their lives. In America, particularly, few people knew enough history or geography to be aware of the facts.

Politicians seized growing sympathy for Europe's Jews as a vehicle for personal aggrandizement. State legislatures in Illinois and New York, where Jews represented large voting blocs, sent memorials to Congress calling for support of a Jewish state in Palestine.

In 1944 the Wright-Compton resolution put before both houses of Congress called upon President Franklin D. Roosevelt to use American power and influence to assure the creation of a Jewish state in Palestine. Secretary of War Henry L. Stimson headed it off by reminding congressional supporters of Zionism that the war was still going on in Arab lands and open United States support for the Zionist cause could endanger the outcome.

The two major political parties paid no heed to Stimson's warning when they were drawing up their 1944 election platforms. Democrats called for "a free and democratic Jewish commonwealth." The Republicans, led by Governor Thomas E. Dewey of New York, substituted the word state for commonwealth.

6: ISRAEL

Birth of an alien state

WHEN thirty thousand Jews in British service were released after World War II, most of them joined the Haganah,
the Jewish Agency's official militia in Palestine, and other extremist Zionist guerilla bands. The abler among them were the
nucleus of an excellent officer corps.

The campaign against the mandate and attacks on Arab centers intensified. On July 22, 1946, Zionists blew up the King
David hotel at Jerusalem and killed a hundred British officials.
British Command Paper 6873, *Statement of Information Relating
to Acts of Violence*, was issued two days later and listed many
terrorist acts committed by Zionist forces. It ended with these
words:

*The evidence contained in the foregoing pages is not, and is not
intended to be, a complete statement of the evidence in the possession of His Majesty's Government. . . .*

*The fact is that in the first six months of 1946 there were nearly
50 separate incidents involving violence, and in many cases loss
of life; material damage to a very great extent has been done to
railroad installations, police and R.A.F. stations, and coast guard
stations. Roads have been mined and vehicles have been blown up.*

*The above operations were widespread in character and caused
very extensive damage. When they were almost immediately followed by the kidnaping of British officers, it was no longer possible
for His Majesty's Government to adopt a passive attitude. Unless
the Government were prepared to yield to threats of violence and*

*to abandon all hope of establishing law and order, they were
bound to take steps against any persons or organizations who had
made themselves responsible for the planning and carrying out of
the outrages which are dealt with in this paper.*

Field Marshal Bernard Montgomery said in his *Memoirs:*

*I had arranged to fly to Palestine on November 28, 1946,
and I faced up to the Prime Minister on the subject [of the Palestine disorders] before my departure. I said that since November
76 soldiers and 23 police had been killed or wounded. Murder and
sabotage were on the increase; rail communication was at a standstill; the Palestine Police Force was 50 percent below strength and
needed 3000 recruits quickly. . . . [T]he general incidence of terrorist activity had increased.*

Britain Gives Up   President Franklin D. Roosevelt does not
appear to have been the Zionist supporter that his family and
partisan politicians later claimed. He never openly favored a
Jewish state. His real attitude seems to have been revealed by
Harold L. Hoskins who, as a special envoy, called upon King
Ibn Saud in 1943. The President's thinking, Hoskins wrote in a
memorandum kept secret until May 1964, "leaned toward a
trusteeship for the Holy Land, with a Jew, a Christian, and a
Moslem as the responsible trustees."[1] One ardent Zionist, Rabbi
Emanuel Neumann, wrote that FDR's "friendship toward
Jews was indisputable, but for the Zionist cause he had little
use and less thought." Roosevelt offered his plan for a Palestine
trusteeship to Josef Stalin and Winston Churchill when the three
met at Tehran. Both rejected it.

Roosevelt died April 12, 1945. Almost before the blossoms
on his grave had lost their fragrance, President Harry S. Truman
reversed United States policy toward Palestine. He had been
president only a week when Secretary of State Edward Stettinius
warned him:

It is very likely that efforts will be made by some of the Zionist leaders to obtain from you at an early date some commitment for unlimited immigration into Palestine and the establishment there of a Jewish state. . . . The question of Palestine is, however, a highly complex one and involves questions which go far beyond the plight of the Jews in Palestine. . . . [A]s we have interests in that area which are vital to the U.S., we feel that this whole subject is one which should be handled with the greatest care and with a view to the long range interests of this country.

Dean Acheson, later to be secretary of state, had a sincere affection for Truman, but he disagreed with the pro-Zionist policy that the president chose to follow:

I did not share the President's view on the Palestine solution to the pressing and desperate plight . . . of displaced Jews in eastern Europe. The number that could be absorbed by Arab Palestine without creating grave political problems would be inadequate, and to transform the country into a Jewish State capable of receiving a million or more immigrants would exacerbate the political problem and imperil not only American but all western interests.[1]

Truman, however, was more politician than statesman. Zionist leaders were pressing him hard, as Stettinius had prophesied, and it was undoubtedly true that Zionist supporters at that time represented in some areas a potentially decisive voting block. Truman urged Prime Minister Clement Attlee of Britain to let one hundred thousand European Jews enter Palestine at once, but Attlee and Foreign Secretary Ernest Bevin refused. They needed Arab good will to save their Arab empire and stuck by the terms of the white paper of May 1939.

Britain was caught in a cleft stick. War had wrecked her economy and revival rested on help from the United States treasury to which Truman held the key. Attlee stalled, proposing an Anglo-American committee of inquiry to study the immigration problem. That body recommended a federal state in Palestine with separate Jewish and Arab regions. Zionists rejected the idea, and Truman went along with the Zionists.

In *A Prime Minister Remembers* Attlee later asserted that United States policy in this period was shaped by the Jewish vote and by large contributions to the Democrats by Zionist supporters. At a Labor Party conference Bevin argued that Truman urged the admission of large numbers of Jews to Palestine because the people of the United States "did not want to allow them into America. . . . The State Department would tell us one thing, then the President would come out with the exact opposite."

Then and thereafter career American diplomats were in continuous turmoil over southwest Asian problems. Men who made foreign affairs a life study looked toward long term objectives. Politicians seeking votes were nearsighted. On October 7, 1946, James Reston wrote in the *New York Times:*

President Truman's [attitude] on Palestine illustrates the influence of domestic politics on U.S. foreign policy and demonstrates the limitations of the theory that politics stops at the water's edge. The general conclusion is that if the Palestine question is approached from the viewpoint of American politics, it is not going to be solved.

The experience of two and a half decades confirms Reston's observation.

Partition   Illegal immigrants were entering Palestine in tens of thousands. They arrived in what Arthur Koestler called little death ships—just about any vessel that would float and some that almost wouldn't. British naval patrols intercepted some and escorted them to Cyprus or turned them back toward Europe. Port authorities ordered some immigrant ships back to sea; often those who had been sent away—and others who never approached an official port—landed secretly on unwatched beaches.

Zionist raids and disorders continued. British officials could preserve no more than a mocking semblance of law and order. On February 18, 1937, Great Britain asked the United Nations to solve the Palestine problem.

The General Assembly named a United Nations Special Committee on Palestine, UNSCOP. From its deliberations emerged two proposals. The minority report, supported by India and three others, recommended a federal Palestinian state with autonomous Jewish and Arab regions. The majority, dominated by western countries, favored separate Jewish and Arab states. The United States backed the majority plan, but the resolution that embodied this program ran into trouble and not until November 29, 1947, could the United States as chief proponent of the scheme muster enough votes to push the measure through the Assembly.[2]

The legal right of an international organization such as the United Nations to dispose of other people's territory in violation of their right of self-determination is still a subject of sharp debate. In practice, however, partition became a historical fact —and the cause of new Arab-Israeli conflict. Under the terms of the partition Jerusalem, a holy city for the three principal religious groups in Palestine, was to be administered by the United Nations as an international enclave open alike to Jew, Christian, and Muslim.[3]

This action ended the British mandate, required Britain to withdraw from Palestine before August 1, 1948, and set up a United Nations Palestine Commission to put partition into effect. There was no reference to self-determination; it was the Zionist's only weak spot.

Arabs everywhere rejected partition. To accept it meant conceding the legality of the Zionist presence and the abandonment of all Arab claims to those areas held by the Zionists. Some Zionists opposed the scheme because it denied them complete control of the country, but David Ben-Gurion, who had succeeded Chaim Weizmann as chief of the Jewish Agency, counseled acceptance. Weizmann, supporting Ben-Gurion, commented that the rest of Palestine "will not be far away."

There were still only 608,000 Jews in Palestine, almost all immigrants, but 1,127,000 native-born Arabs outnumbering Jews almost two to one. Jews owned only six percent of the land area.[4]

Nevertheless, partition gave the Jewish state over fifty percent of Palestine, including most of the shore line of Lake Tiberias. The north shore was to be a demilitarized area to which Arab farmers in Syria would have access. The Zionist state would also get virtually all of the best farmland and best ports. The Arab state was to consist of two unconnected regions, one embracing the Gaza Strip and part of the Sinai border area, the other a portion of the west bank of the Jordan River. It was impossible for the Jewish state to have a homogeneous population because in the Zionist region the number of Arab inhabitants was within a few thousand of the number of Jews. This fact alone was a harbinger of certain conflict. Thus the Palestinians had to be removed.

Partition: The United States Role   After he left office, President Truman wrote, "I have never approved of the practice of the strong imposing their will on the weak whether among men or among nations." He did not, however, let that interfere with his decision to force Zionist rule on Palestine. Dean Acheson's disagreement with him has already been reported. Other members of his government revealed the manner in which he used American power to get partition approved. Said Sumner Welles, undersecretary of state:

By direct order of the White House every form of pressure, direct or indirect, was brought to bear by American officials upon those countries outside the Moslem world that were known to be either uncertain or opposed to partitions. Representatives or intermediaries were employed by the White House to make sure that the necessary majority would at least be assured.[5]

Secretary of Defense James Forrestal lamented the consequences of the Truman policy in Arab countries:

*America has lost very greatly in prestige in the Arab world. . . .
The methods that had been used to bring coercion and duress on
other nations in the General Assembly bordered closely onto
scandal.*[6]

In its issue of October 15, 1951, *Time* reviewed Forrestal's
Diaries:

*All-out support of a Zionist state, he believed, was fraught
with great danger for the security of the country. Democratic
National Chairman J. Howard McGrath gravely warned him that
the Democrats would probably lose the States of New York,
Pennsylvania and California if they did not heed Zionist ambitions.
As Forrestal had foreseen, all-out. U.S. support of Israel left scars
of hatred and distrust of the United States in the Arab world.*

Explaining the position of the United States is Harry Truman's statement in his memoirs about having several million
Jews in his constituency but no Arabs. This pragmatic cynicism
so often displayed by America's leaders left its indelible marks
on the Arabs. America's government cannot be trusted.

And So to War   Since 1945 the Arab League had warned
that any attempt to set up a Zionist state in Palestine meant war,
but in the west only Britain appears to have recognized the
seriousness of that danger. Ordered to be out of Palestine by
August, the British said they would leave by May 15, 1948.
Meanwhile they would bar from Palestine any United Nations
agency sent to prepare the way for partition.

Britain withdrew on May 14. A provisional government at
Tel Aviv proclaimed the State of Israel. Mere minutes later
Truman extended diplomatic recognition. Some years later
students at the University of Cairo asked a visiting United
States newsman to cite even one example of such precipitate
action by an American government. He could not. In the whole

sweep of United States diplomatic history there was no precedent.

Egypt, Transjordan, Syria, Lebanon, and Iraq sent armed units into Palestine to smash the embryonic state, and at first it seemed they might succeed. Transjordan's Arab Legion, the most competent and best led army in the Arab world, seized most of the west bank of the Jordan River and the old city of Jerusalem. Syria blocked the Israelis from the north shore of Lake Tiberias, known in the Bible as the Sea of Galilee. Egypt grabbed the Gaza Strip on the Mediterranean coast. Lebanon's weak little army did nothing at all. Iraqi troops reinforced the Transjordanian units in the east.

One day after the British withdrawal the United Nations General Assembly sent Count Folke Bernadotte, chairman of the Swedish Red Cross, to try to stop the fighting. He negotiated feeble truces that both sides soon broke.

The Zionists grew stronger. Haganah was already an experienced army with the thirty thousand Jews who had served in the British ranks. Western volunteers, mainly Americans, almost all veterans of the recent world war, offered their services. Israel now had almost unlimited access to western arms and supplies.

The Arabs were in poorer case. The Arab Legion fought the Zionists to a standstill in their area, but it was too small to operate on a wider front. France had been careful not to let the Syrians, while they were under her control, build an army strong enough to stage a rebellion. For the same reason Great Britain had kept Iraqi and Egyptian forces poorly armed, poorly led, and inadequately trained.

On September 18 Bernadotte dispatched his last report to the secretary general of the United Nations. On September 19 Stern Gang gunmen killed him in Jerusalem. The Assembly then sent an American, Ralph Bunche, who worked out new truces between Israel and the Arab states on a country-to-country basis. These agreements stipulated that each army was to retain possession of the territory it then occupied.

Israel violated every one of the agreements. The most important, historically, was seizure of the Arab village of Umm Rashrash, on the Gulf of Aqaba. In Israeli hands Umm Rashrash became the port of Eilat, Israel's only opening onto the Gulf of Aqaba and part of her justification for an attack against Egypt in 1967.

7: THE PALESTINIAN DIASPORA

The fate of the first million refugees

IN DECEMBER 1947 after the United Nations had decided on partition, "a senior officer in the Arab Legion was one day visiting a British district officer in Palestine," reports General John Bagot Glubb.[1] A Jewish district officer of the mandate authority was present. One of the Britons noted that the Jewish state as mapped would be populated almost equally by Jews and Arabs. He wondered what troubles such a division might cause. "That will be fixed," the Jewish officer said, "a few calculated massacres will get rid of them."

Just such a solution was being adopted even before Great Britain left Palestine. In January 1948 Zionists used dynamite to kill twenty-two Palestinians and wound many more in the public square at Jaffa. The next day Zionists blew up the Semiramis hotel at Jerusalem and twenty-two more Arabs died. There were many other such attacks. The worst was at Deir Yasin. The whole village was destroyed while its inhabitants slept; all 257 men, women, and children were killed. All Arabs in the village of Beit al Khouri were killed. In April Zionist forces occupied Tiberias and Tamakh, took Haifa and Jaffa, and occupied the Arab quarter of Katamon in Jerusalem. Safad was taken May 10, Beisan May 11, Akka on May 14.

After May 14 hundreds of thousands of Palestinians fled in fear from areas held or threatened by the Israelis. Zionist forces expelled as many more but later argued that all these people were voluntary refugees. Arab political and military leaders, they said, had advised Arab civilians to leave. This false claim was still being repeated in the United States at the end of 1970. The British Broadcasting Corporation monitored every radio message transmitted from and to the areas of the fighting, and an exhaustive study of BBC records made by British writer Erskine Childers found not one instance in which Arab leaders had urged civilians to flee.

I. F. Stone writing in the *New York Review of Books* declared:

Jewish terrorism, not only by the Irgun in such savage massacres as Deir Yasin but in milder form by the Haganah itself "encouraged" Arabs to leave areas the Jews wished to take over for strategic or demographic reasons. They tried to make as much of Israel as free of Arabs as possible.

These were precisely the tactics prophesied by the Jewish district officer quoted by Glubb. That pattern was still being followed by the Israeli government more than eight years later.

Arnold Toynbee commented:

The evil deeds committed by the Zionist Jews . . . were comparable to crimes committed against the Jews by the Nazis. . . . [The Arab-blood bath] at Deir Yasin was on the head of the Irgun; the expulsions after the 15th of May, 1948, were on the heads of all Israel.[2]

Jon Kimche, a British Zionist, confessed that "(t)he massacre at Deir Yasin was the darkest blot on the Jewish record throughout all the fighting."[3] Official records and the historical writings of many men abound in similar reports and comment.

Bernadotte   No one will ever know how many Palestinian men, women, and children were killed during this period. Even the numbers of those who fled their homes or were driven into exile are an approximation. In 1947 there were more than a million Christian and Muslim Arabs in Palestine; after June 1948 the Arabs remaining in Israel were only a handful. Most victims of the Palestinian diaspora found refuge in Transjordan or the Gaza Strip, then held by Egypt. Others reached Lebanon and Syria. Some got to Iraq.

The host nations were too poor to absorb and feed large numbers of new residents. The United Nations Relief and Works Agency (UNRWA) assumed responsibility for their care. UNRWA's funds came from money donated by a few countries. Those gifts amounted to seven cents per person per day for shelter, food, clothing, medical care, and education. By 1971 this sum had risen to eleven cents.[4]

In his last report to the United Nations Bernadotte expressed his ideas of what a Palestine peace must include:

It is not yet known what the policy of the Provisional Government of Israel with regard to the return of the refugees will be when the final terms of settlement are reached. It is, however, undeniable that no settlement can be just and complete if recognition is not accorded to the right of the refugee to return to the home from which he has been dislodged by the hazards and strategy of the armed conflict between Arabs and Jews in Palestine. It would be an offense against the principle of elemental justice if these innocent victims of the conflict were denied the right of return to their homes while Jewish immigrants flow into Palestine, and, indeed, at least offer the threat of permanent replacement of the Arab refugees who have been rooted in the land for centuries.

He also commented on Zionist looting and destruction of Arab villages:

The liability of the Provisional Government of Israel to restore private property to its Arab owners and to indemnify those owners for property wantonly destroyed is clear.... But in any case their unconditional right to make a free choice should be fully respected.

Bernadotte's goal was peace, and he submitted his own plan, which the General Assembly ignored, for the partition of Palestine. He concluded his report with these words:

The Jewish State was not born in peace as was hoped for in the resolution of November 29, 1947, but rather in bloodshed and violence.

Refugees: 1945 and 1949   In 1945 hundreds of thousands of refugees from Nazi tyranny filled camps in Europe. Most were European Jews. In 1949 seven hundred thousand Palestinians lived in camps in Syria, Lebanon, Transjordan, and Egypt. All were Christian or Muslim Arabs. In 1945 the west, led by the United States, donated huge sums for housing and feeding European refugees. In 1949 the west did very little. The comparison is a matter of historical record and reflects small credit on western Christendom. West Germany under heavy pressure from the United States paid huge reparations to Jews and to Israel for nazi terrorism. Israel did nothing whatever to sustain or compensate the Palestinians, and the United States never prodded her to meet any part of this obligation.

Israel tried to evade her responsibility by pleading that Arab host states were not doing enough for the refugees. John Davis, for five years the American commissioner of UNRWA, contradicted this claim, insisting that the Arab host states were giving the refugees all the help they could and had already absorbed so many of them.

By 1967 UNRWA reported more than 1.35 million on the refugee rolls. Davis said:

The simple truth is that the jobs at which the refugees could be employed do not exist today within the host countries. Nor could any large number of jobs be created within these countries . . .

because of the limited local resources and scope of employment.
[He went on,] *The refugee host countries . . . have themselves
been generous and hospitable to the refugees. In terms of direct
assistance, they have spent more than $100,000,000,* [as of 1960.
The total by 1971 was far greater.] *mostly for education, health
services, camp sites, housing, road improvement and the maintenance of security. . . . Contrary to much western thinking, the
Arab host Governments have also helped qualified young refugees
to obtain employment in the host countries and elsewhere.*

Israel and the Refugees   At its autumn session in 1948 the
United Nations Assembly wrote Bernadotte's recommendations
for the repatriation and/or compensation of the Palestinians
into a resolution adopted without opposition. It called upon
Israel to permit all Palestinians to return to their homes and to
compensate any who chose not to go back. Once each year
for twenty years that resolution was re-adopted by unanimous
vote. It accomplished nothing.[5]

Meanwhile Israel was vigorously campaigning throughout the
world for Jewish immigrants. Israel's once 608 thousand Jews
in 1948 had become 3 million in 1971. More were urged to come
although there was no room for the original people, the Palestinians.

In the camps Palestinian bitterness increased. The chief of the
UNRWA mission, Dr. Laurence Michelmore, reported:

*[The refugees] feel that they have been betrayed, and their resent-
ment is directed not only against those whom they regard as the
chief authors of their exile but also against the international community at large, whom they hold responsible for the partition of
their homeland, which they regard against natural justice.[6]*

"Sometimes," a *New York Times* writer said, "the United
States comes first in their enmity. Israel they regard as the chief
antagonist, but the United States to them is Israel's chief shield
and sustenance."[7]

United States Attitudes   The United States was the largest contributor to UNRWA funds, but at the same time Washington did whatever it could to advance Israel's claims. One scheme involved Habib Bourguiba, president of Tunisia, in an effort to divide the Arab states on the issue of Israel and the Palestinians. Early in 1963 Bourguiba proposed that the Arab countries negotiate a settlement with Israel of the refugee problem. Abba Eban, the articulate statesman and foreign minister of Israel, responded in *Foreign Affairs* with an essay encouraging payment of compensation to resettle the Arab refugees.[8]

Many observers concluded that Bourguiba's speech and Eban's essay had been coordinated at Washington before they appeared. Their almost simultaneous appearance could of course have been mere coincidence, but that seems altogether unlikely. Matters seldom take place in that fashion on important international issues. It seems reasonably certain that Bourguiba knew what Eban would say before be spoke and that Eban knew what Bourguiba would say before he spoke. The mechanics of writing a careful essay on such a question and the routine work involved in editing, printing, and circulating a scholarly magazine support this skeptical conclusion.

Other circumstances bolster this judgment. Bourguiba was the one Arab leader whom the United States might have enlisted in such a project. Moreover, *Foreign Affairs* is known to have been a willing transmission-belt for views that Washington wanted published without attribution to any official source. Of this there are several examples, including an essay on Soviet-American relations by a Mr. X, who turned out to be George F. Kennan, ambassador to USSR, and a piece on Vietnam by George Carter, a member of the Central Intelligence Agency. The exchange between Bourguiba and Eban would therefore seem to have been prearranged in the United States Department of State.

In every other Arab land leaders denounced Bourguiba as a traitor. Whatever usefulness he might once have had as a spokes-

man for the west was dead. Of his plan to recognize Israel and
Eban's dream to resettle the Palestinians in far regions the
world heard no more.

Palestinians: Refugees or a Nation?   Western peoples—even,
indeed, Arab leaders and the Israelis—seemed to ignore a glar-
ing fact—the war for Palestine began as a struggle between
Palestinians and Zionist immigrants for possession of the narrow
strip of land that is now Israel. That struggle remained despite
the ancillary conflicts that troubled the Arab region. Even as
late as 1967 when the United Nations adopted its resolution
242 to bring peace to the Middle East, it referred to the Palestinian people as "refugees" and gave them no voice in the
determination of their fate.

In 1948 neighboring Arab states intervened in the Palestine
war but they were never the principal actors. Truces between
Egypt or Jordan and Israel—even a formal peace treaty to
which these governments could be parties—can never be effective without the voluntary participation of the principal parties,
the Palestinians.

For over twenty years the whole world spoke of the dislodged
Palestinians only as refugees, but one hears that phrase less
frequently now. In Israel and the United States, however,
official attitudes and policies seemed to be based on a refugee
syndrome.

The Zionists (and the United States government) hoped that
the refugee problem could be wished away—that the Palestinians would consent to their removal from the borders of their
homeland to distant districts of the Arab world where, like the
French Acadians of Nova Scotia, they would settle down to a
new and peaceful existence. The trouble has been that the
Zionists and their American allies accepted their own wish as
ordained fact.

Millions of people and most of the governments of the world
have begun to accept the validity of the Palestinian attitude. If,

as Zionists claim, the Jews of the earth nourished a dream of a reconstituted Israel in Palestine through eighteen hundred years, is it not unrealistic to believe that Palestinian Arabs would abandon hope for a return to their own land just beyond a river bank or just across an imaginary line?

Jews had ruled a kingdom there barely seven decades out of this entire period. Arabs have ruled Palestine for thirteen centuries, as they had inhabited it even prior to the almost three thousand years of recorded history. The Arab name for the country is derived from the Philistines, a people whose land the Jews under Joshua invaded after the death of Moses. But it took the 1967 war, the Palestinian commandos and their exploits, to finally come to grips with the existence of a Palestinian people entity.

her, presented a resolution demanding that all foreign troops leave Egypt forthwith. Belgium moved to eliminate "forthwith," which would mean the invaders could set their own schedule for getting out of Egypt, and there would be time to negotiate some kind of settlement that would save face.

Winthrop Aldrich reports that Henry Cabot Lodge, United States ambassador to the United Nations, had orders from Secretary Dulles to support the Belgian amendment and, if that move failed, to abstain from voting on the Indian resolution.[9] However, Lodge appears to have voted in obedience to conscience rather than orders. He abstained from voting on the Belgian amendment and next day cast the United States ballot in support of the Indian resolution. This was the first time on record that American representatives in the United Nations had supported the Arab position or voted against a Zionist-Israeli program.

Later American spokesmen claimed exclusive credit for the end of the three-state aggression. The facts refute them, and certainly no Arab state credits their claim. The USSR, on the other hand, won new respect and prestige in the Arab world.

British domestic problems and his diplomatic defeat in the United Nations persuaded Eden that his gamble had failed. Egypt blocked the canal as Bulganin had warned, and no oil got through. Syrian troops blew up the pipeline that carried Iraqi oil across their country. Western Europe depended on Arab oil for twenty percent of its total power needs, and earth offered no adequate alternative source of the desperately needed petroleum.[10]

Britain tried rationing oil, and United States firms made a gesture by diverting a few cargoes of western hemisphere oil to Europe. But eighty percent of Europe's petroleum came from the Arab world, and when that oil stopped flowing, western Europe suffered grievously.

Before January 1, 1957, France and Britain were gone from Egypt and the Suez Canal was being cleared. Israel's expansionism presented a more stubborn problem; Zionist planners had always intended that Sinai should be part of their theocratic state. Reluctantly, under United States pressure Ben-Gurion agreed to evacuate Sinai, but he refused to leave Gaza or Sharm al Sheik until Dulles threatened to cut off all American aid to Israel. The United States sent a ship through the Strait of Tiran to Eilat, and Israel for the first time had direct access to the Red Sea enabling her to import urgently needed oil from Iran.

A United Nations Emergency Force (UNEF) provided by several countries was to be stationed ostensibly on both sides of the Israeli-Egyptian border. Nasser agreed to let units occupy posts in Sinai and at Sharm al Sheik, but Israel refused to let any foreign soldiers cross her frontier, and the UN took no action to require her to admit them.

These facts have special significance in subsequent history. UNEF entered Egypt not under force of law but only with Egypt's express permission because the United Nations possessed neither the power nor the authority to impose the presence of troops. The position was that of a guest at sufferance who, when the owner's permission to be on his land is withdrawn, must leave.

Israel had hoped that the United States could also compel Egypt to open the Suez to her shipping, but the canal remained an Egyptian waterway which only the rest of the world could use. Although a United Nations resolution called upon Egypt to let the Israelis use the canal, Nasser took the position that his country could hardly be expected to obey this resolution while Israel continued to ignore the many United Nations orders addressed to her.

Empires Die   The failure of their Suez gamble set off a chain of military and political disasters for the British and the French in the Arab world. America's repeated attempts to rescue her European allies from the consequences of their folly and weakness fastened a pattern of Arab hostility which still faces the United States. No Arab can be expected to forget, either, that it was John Foster Dulles who precipitated the 1956 Suez crisis with his clumsy management of the Aswan High Dam affair.

As earlier noted, there had long been sharp disagreement on United States policy in the Arab world between diplomats in the field and politicians at home. Envoys assigned in the area as well as experts in the lower echelons of the state department, for whom international affairs were a career and a lifetime study, knew and repeatedly argued that Israel's aims and ambitions directly contravened America's long term interests at almost every point. Those politicans who dictated policy were primarily concerned with local voting patterns in the United States and their own prospects in the next election. These considerations made them subject to pro-Israel pressures.

American attitudes toward the USSR and communism were another factor. One American goal was to shut the Soviets out of the strategically and economically vital southwest Asian region. However, the Aswan Dam affair and the confrontation at Suez had reduced that policy to a shambles. Now the United States itself faced the risk of exclusion.

At the Bandung (Indonesia) conference of Asian and African states in 1955 the first bloc of anti-imperialist countries had begun to take form. As new states emerged from European colonialism, they formed a bloc which acquired vital importance in world affairs. The Bandung group as such disintegrated, but its members continued to voice and to vote their antiwesternism. What emerged was the concept of nonalignment, which was to survive its main protagonists, Nehru, Nasser, and Tito.

Meanwhile, at Aswan the harnessed waters of Lake Nasser permitted irrigation of two million acres that had lain empty and barren. Steel mills light the night sky. Fertilizer plants furnish nutrients for the soil. Other industries are developing. In several areas oil has been discovered.

Egypt is still economically developing, and emphasis on needed industry and military commitments withholds from the people many benefits that might otherwise have been available to them. However Egypt has become a relatively self-sustaining country for the first time since Muhammad Ali.

12: JORDAN

An uneasy crown

JORDAN has little to offer the world but a colorful past. The ancient Hebrew patriarch Abraham died here. Moses, the Bible tells us, struck water from the rocks of these barren hills. Storied Babylon ruled this region. So, too, did Greece and Rome. The Greek city of Philadelphia occupied the site on which Amman now stands, and Marc Anthony delivered the red rock city of Petra to Cleopatra as a token of his love. Crusading Arabs defeated Byzantine legions on the banks of the Yarmuk and opened Palestine and Syria to the new nation of Islam. In World War I the legendary Lawrence of Arabia and Sheik Auda abu Tayi crushed the Turks here and captured Aqaba, now Jordan's only seaport.

This region called Jordan had been for many centuries part of Palestine*, a portion of the realm that Sherif Hussein of Mecca expected to be the Arab kingdom which Britain had promised for his help against Turkey. The British kept it all for themselves. The chiefs of Syria chose Hussein's son Faisal to be their king. When the League of Nations gave Syria to France under a mandate, Faisal refused to acknowledge French authority, and French troops expelled him. In February 1921 his elder brother Abdullah gathered an army of desert Arabs and set out to reestablish Faisal's throne. He got only as far as Amman, where Colonial Secretary Winston Churchill intercepted him and offered a deal.

* See note on page 23.

The Balfour Declaration was still new and Jewish immigration to Palestine was only a trickle, but British officials were already growing skeptical of the possible consequences. In Mesopotamia bitter Arabs were already in full revolt. In every Arab land resentment was growing against the Zionists and their plan.

Britain hoped to limit the Zionist danger and soothe native anger by dividing Palestine at the banks of the Jordan River, calling the eastern region Transjordan.[1] She named Abdullah the ruler of a new emirate there, established his capital at Amman, and promised him a subsidy of $24 million per year to sustain his regime. The terms of the Balfour Declaration, London decreed, did not apply to Transjordan therefore no Jewish immigrant would be admitted to that region. When the League of Nations got around to approving a Palestine mandate, Transjordan was recognized as British territory and the mandate applied only to that part of Palestine west of the Jordan River.[2]

The Arab Region   Transjordan's natural resources consisted of almost nothing except the rich farming land of the river valley and the still unexploited—indeed, untested—mineral treasures of the Dead Sea. Farmers constituted a minority of her three hundred thousand population and the others were tribal nomads roaming the eastern desert.

The emirate was just another British satrapy. British advisers managed every government department. Secure in their control of the country, the British raised and trained a small but very able and mobile army to keep the Zionists on their side of the river and block French expansion eastward from Syria. This new Arab Legion drew all its native members from the bedouin tribes. It was by far the best, most efficient native army in the Arab world.

Before 1915 a Turkish-owned railway had ferried Muslim pilgrims across this region to and from the holy cities of Medina and Mecca, but British and Arab troops destroyed the line to hamper the transfer of enemy troops. After the war the railway remained in rusting disuse because Britain, France, and Turkey could not agree on its ownership and operation.

Palestine   By 1945 Arabs everywhere were demanding freedom from their European masters. Egypt and Iraq had nominal independence but it was not real and not satisfying. Transjordan, too, wanted to manage its own affairs even though it was obvious that the little country could not possibly stand alone.

In 1946 Great Britain proclaimed Transjordan a sovereign state*, but its freedom was not even a plausible pretense. The dinar was tied to the British pound; British officers continued to command Transjordan's small armed forces; British advisers determined the course of her international affairs. In name Emir Abdullah was an absolute monarch, but in practice he had almost no power at all.

In May 1948 the Arab Legion led by General John Bagot Glubb crossed the river into Palestine and occupied Judea, Samaria, and northern Negev, plus the old and sacred section of Jerusalem. The 1948 armistice agreement put Abdullah into possession of most of the west bank of the Jordan River. He took the title of king and changed the name of his realm to The Hashimite Kingdom of Jordan. He annexed the West Bank area—and thereby incurred the anger of other Arab rulers as well as the West Bank residents, who counted themselves still Palestinians. He had enlarged his territory by a third and the number of his subjects to 1.2 million.

Since the time of Solomon or before, the river had formed a natural boundary between the settled agricultural west and the sparsely peopled eastern desert. Now Abdullah claimed power over the west bank farmers and some seven hundred thousand other Palestinians who had fled or been expelled from the Zionist-occupied areas. All his new subjects were people who had lived in fixed abodes for thirteen hundred years or more,

* The "independence" accorded to Jordan was intended chiefly to give Britain a free hand in that state but relieve her of international responsibility for the actions of the Jordanian government.

men of the soil, artisans, craftsmen, and merchants, totally different in background and attitudes from the tribal nomads he had learned to rule. To bring these disparate peoples together under one weak and penniless government—one group three times as large as the other—posed a problem that he and his successors could not hope to solve. His reliance upon the tribesmen, whose ways he understood, to maintain his government aroused a natural resentment among the new Palestinian majority who had neither role nor voice in Jordanian affairs.

Farmer and Nomad   The inevitable antagonism between men who lead settled lives and those who rove from place to place had special significance in Jordan. Through tens of generations the customs and attitudes of Palestinian farmer and bedouin herdsman had grown far apart. Their social systems were as unlike as those of Kansas farmers and plains Indians.

For the farmer land was a close, intimate part of his life. His fathers' fathers and their fathers before them had tilled these same dunums into which he thrust his plow at planting time. He had an almost holy affection for his soil, and his own roots went more deeply into the land than the roots of his olive trees.

For men of the desert the land was an open reach that ran forever away toward far horizons. They loved it, too, but as a seafarer loves the limitless waters of the ocean. The land belonged to him who was there. It provided pasture for his beasts and made no effort to hold him back when the pursuit of water or forage sent him to seek a new scene. The land was something to fiercely fight for.

In Palestine traditional tribalism had long vanished since it served no economic or political purpose. Councils of family patriarchs managed village affairs. Because each family had its identifiable patch to till, the system of feudal tenure brought in by the Turks gave neither reason nor opportunity for intercommunity quarrels. Therefore the circumstances that make for war did not exist. But not all Palestinians were farmers. Many were excellent artisans. Others were merchants and traders who traveled by sea and caravan into neighboring Arab countries to buy and sell.

Farmer, artisan, merchant, and nomad were all Arabs. Most accepted the law of the Koran, but they were not and could not be one people. Emir Abdullah was a desert prince whose authority rested upon the loyalty of desert men, and he kept desert sheiks about him to advise and protect him. The western Palestinians now within his realm resented the preferential status of the three hundred thousand bedouin. They hated Israel for the rape of their homeland. They hated Great Britain for making the Zionist invasion of Palestine possible; and they hated the United States for making the political and economic existence of Israel feasible.

Israel hoped that she could persuade or compel Jordan and the Palestinians to accept her presence. Time after time she demanded direct negotiation with the Arab states as a basis for peace. To the western world Israel's way became the way of reason. Israel's attempt to trade military superiority for legitimacy made any reasonable settlement impossible.

The Arabs rejected the Israeli proposals on sound legal grounds. A treaty between nations constitutes recognition by each of the other's legal and political right to deal as a sovereign state with the matters at issue. None of Israel's Arab neighbors would acknowledge the Zionist claim to a lawful national existence or to de jure political authority over one square inch of Arab territory. No Arab state could dare antagonize its own people by dealing with an intransigent, dominant Israel.

Not all Arab governments pursued this policy with equal enthusiasm, but none (except Tunisia for a short time) rejected it. The one weak link in the Arab chain around Palestine had been Jordan. Abdullah had only his British subsidy to keep his emirate alive and dared not defy his western sponsors. The United States and Britain forced him into a secret deal with Israel. On July 20, 1951, a Palestinian nationalist shot him to death in a Jerusalem mosque.

Crown Prince Tallal was a patient in a Swiss clinic. Rumors

were that he was vigorously anti-British and that his first act as king would be to drive every British official from Jordan. The puppet parliament, which had no constitutional authority to do so, deposed Tallal on the ground of mental incompetence and passed the crown to his son Hussein. Then a fifteen-year-old schoolboy Hussein was in England being trained in the ways that Great Britain believed an Arab king should go.

The Palestinians   Jordan now claimed rule over 1.2 million people in a land that could not have fed more than a third as many. The state had no industry and nothing on which industry could be based. Its only path to the sea ran through the tiny port of Aqaba, which had neither rail nor road to connect it with the rest of the country. The United Nations had ordered Israel to let Jordan use Haifa, but yielding to U.N. orders was not a common Israeli practice.

The Palestinians were bitter men. They threw their support to the Communists, the Muslim Brotherhood, and the Arab socialist party Baath. None supported the monarchy.

At eighteen Hussein began to rule in his own name. He tried to mollify the Palestinians by making them full citizens, and proclaimed a constitution which in fact whittled away not one iota of his absolute authority. As discontent grew, he banned all existing political parties and set harsh rules for creating new ones. He jailed opposition leaders, called elections, and had his police make sure that the ballots were counted as he would have them. The Palestinians responded with violent demonstrations.

Relations with other Arab states and the conduct of foreign affairs were colored by domestic issues. The nature of Jordan's existence made her an international political shuttlecock. The West Bank Palestinians were her biggest problem. They honored nobody; their foes were Israel and the western powers upon whom both Israel and King Hussein relied for support.

Jordan's border was long and indefensible, and the west denied Hussein enough arms to maintain an adequate army. Nor could he have found enough Jordanian tribesmen to fill

145358

EMORY & HENRY LIBRARY

out expanded ranks. His only alternative would have been to enlist Palestinians, whose loyalty was at best doubtful.

Israel took advantage of this situation. As the Arab revolution heightened the young king's internal risks, Israel multiplied the number and the severity of her border raids. Hussein's inability to counter them added to his domestic woes. In December 1953 Israeli troops wiped out the village of Kibya, then razed Nabhalin. Other such incidents took place, and in every case investigated by the United Nations Israel was found at fault. Jordan's interior minister spoke out bitterly, reflecting the belief held by all Arabs.

Israel fights with American aid. It takes money to buy American ammunition like that found at Kibya and Nabhalin. America feeds her creation Israel and makes no effort to restrain that creation from frontier attacks.[3]

METO   The Truman-Acheson regime had created a North Atlantic Treaty Organization (NATO) as a political, economic, and military barrier against the Soviet Union in Europe. Secretary of State John Foster Dulles undertook to erect a similar barrier in southwest Asia. He enlisted Turkey, Pakistan, and Iraq. It is fully discussed in a later chapter. He drew a reluctant Great Britain and a hesitant Iran into the plan, and established a Middle East Treaty Organization (METO) with headquarters at Baghdad.

The United States wanted Jordan in METO but could not promise that the new alliance or any of its members would protect the little kingdom from Israel. METO was designed to advance United States interests in the Arab lands. Hussein agreed to enlist, but the violent opposition of his Palestinian subjects and some of his ministers forced him to back off. When the Arab League discussed METO, Hussein's own foreign minister denounced the scheme, then fled for his life to safety in Syria.

Even then, with a new cabinet in office Hussein seemed determined to sign the Baghdad treaty, but every one of his ministers resigned. At Amman angry mobs assaulted the United States consulate. Hussein ordered new elections, and the opposition won enough seats to force the appointment as prime minister of Suleiman Nabulsi, who was opposed to a western alliance. Nabulsi renounced the alliance with Britain and ordered every British official out of the country.

The Eisenhower Doctrine In March 1957 the United States Congress authorized President Eisenhower to intervene with military force wherever any state that was threatened by international communism requested such help. Iraq, Lebanon, and Libya announced their acceptance of the program, and again King Hussein wanted to sign up. Once more internal opposition thwarted him; civilians demonstrated; some of his handpicked bedouin officers mutinied. The United States Sixth Fleet paraded past the Lebanese coast a few minutes flying time from Amman, and Hussein was awarded $40 million in U.S. aid. The king survived but he did not endorse the Eisenhower Doctrine.

Arab kings watched the advance of the revolution fearfully. Jordan, Iraq, and Saudi Arabia signed a King's Alliance that died in its birth throes. Jordan and Iraq, whose kings were cousins, created an Arab Federation to counter the new United Arab Republic formed by Egypt and Syria. Under this federation the two young monarchs were to take turns serving as paramount king, but Hussein's turn did not come. King Faisal II of Iraq died when Brigadier Abdul Karim Kassem destroyed the Iraqi monarchy.

Es Samu The Jordan River was desperately important to both Jordan and Israel. Each needed as much river water as it could get for irrigation. With American financial help Israel built a huge pumping and irrigation system and began to divert the river's flow far beyond the Jordan River valley into her Negev desert region. Under a water plan approved by the Arab League Syria began to dig a canal that was to carry the flow of the Banias River, a Jordan tributary, directly into Hussein's kingdom. The scheme had a double purpose, to give Jordanians the water they needed and to reduce the flow available to Israel from the river's natural reservoir in Lake Tiberias. Israeli guns and planes attacked the Syrian project and brought it to a halt.

Meanwhile Palestinian guerillas were increasing the number and severity of their raids into Israel. On Sunday, November 13, 1966, Israeli troops in brigade strength struck the West Bank village of Es Samu and two hamlets, all inhabited solely by Palestinians. United Nations investigators reported the destruction of 125 buildings, the death of 18 people, and the wounding of 27.[4]

The Arab states, supported by other Asians and Africans, called Israel before the United Nations Security Council. Not even the United States delegate—himself an ardent Zionist—dared to justify or defend the Israeli attack, and the Council voted the strongest resolution of censure it had ever adopted against any state.

Israel had used the Palestinians' raids into her territory as an excuse for her attacks upon Jordan, and now those attacks increased. The Palestinians condemned Hussein for failing to protect the people he claimed to rule. Hoping to quiet their criticism, he promised to arm the Palestinians so that they might participate in their own defense. The pledge was not kept. Hussein did not have and could not get arms for so many. In any event, arming the Palestinians at that point in time would merely have increased his own danger.

Hussein was not, however, merely a western stooge. He was first an Arab, an Arab nationalist, as eager as any man to dispose of the Zionist menace. He was a harassed, lonely, young ruler in an impossible situation, caught in a clash of forces that he could neither control nor even cope with.[5] He opposed the Arab revolution because his throne and perhaps his life depended upon resistance, but ultimately the Palestinian liberation movement and the forward thrust of the Arab revolution would engulf him and most of what he stood for.

13: SYRIA

The old and the new
in conflict

THE WEST was at war. Coventry's cathedral was rubble. Bomb and flame tore great gaps in London. Poland had become a German province. In France a senile marshal and a scheming politician reigned at Vichy under Nazi rule. At Beirut the governor general gave his allegiance to Vichy, and a German-Italian delegation set up shop at Damascus to foment disorders in Britain's Arab lands.

In June 1941 an Anglo-French army drove into Syria and Lebanon from Palestine and Transjordan. Charles de Gaulle, chief of a French exile regime at London, demanded that Syria and Lebanon be surrendered to his control. Taking over rule of those lands was General Georges Catroux, who proclaimed both Syria and Lebanon sovereign states and named dependable native stooges to govern each country.

Arabs there had been trying since 1919 to oust the French. Nationalists in both states demanded free elections. De Gaulle and Catroux stalled. The De Gaulle of 1941 was still a stubborn imperialist, no more eager than Winston Churchill to set subject peoples free.

One political party, the National Bloc, had been Syria's chief spokesman for independence in the time between the two world wars. Now the Bloc became active again. Protests and demonstrations finally persuaded De Gaulle to dust off the provisional constitutions drawn up before World War II but never used.

Elections held in Syria in 1942 gave the Bloc a huge majority in the new House of Deputies, but Syria still was not allowed to govern herself.[1]

The French high commissioner had power to suspend constitutional guarantees, prorogue the legislature, and rule by decree. He commanded native military forces, had sole authority over foreign affairs, and collected the customs. He could censor, suspend, or prohibit all publications. He rejected the claim for independence because, he argued, only the League of Nations, author of the French mandate, could withdraw it.

In Great Britain Parliament had made Churchill a virtual dictator. He meant to restore and preserve his king's colonial empire, and he still entertained the ambition of earlier governments to substitute British for French authority where France ruled in the Arab world. Unstable conditions in Syria, he warned De Gaulle, posed a threat to the allied war effort in the Arab regions.

To counteract unsettled conditions Catroux gave a hasty pledge of freedom for Lebanon and Syria. When this resulted in his recall by De Gaulle, Winston Churchill and President Franklin D. Roosevelt (who shared Churchill's personal dislike for the French leader) demanded that Catroux be returned to his post with new promises of independence.

The time was gone, however, when the peoples of the Arab world could be fobbed off with words. In 1944 the Syrian House of Deputies made a ceremony of its refusal to mention France or the mandate in the oath.

On May 17, 1945, France sent a new contingent of Senegalese troops into Syria. They were only in transit, Paris said, but whither they were bound and when they would leave were not revealed. Strikes strangled Beirut, Tripoli, and Damascus.

Syria and Lebanon had joined the Arab League in March. Now they dismissed every Frenchman who held any government post and seized control of the internal security forces, the Special Troops. New riots exploded in every major city and town, and on May 29 French planes bombarded Damascus. Five hundred Arab civilians died.

British troops, who had been in the country since 1941, received orders from London to drive the French back to their billets. Syria and Lebanon demanded withdrawal of all foreign forces, British as well as French. Because the Europeans would set no timetable for getting out, Damascus and Beirut took the issue to the new United Nations.

In the Security Council the United States, Britain, and France dominated. The United States offered a resolution of confidence that the Europeans would depart "as soon as practicable," without a definition of practicable. The measure won enough votes for passage but a Soviet veto killed it. London and Paris confessed defeat. By May 1946 all foreign troops were gone from Syria and the last French soldier left Lebanon before the end of the year.

The Old and the New   Revolution is a continuing struggle between what has been and what must be, between a system no longer able to serve man's needs and one that offers something better. While the old imposes its power, the new cannot be born, and people may turn to violence to make the birth possible.

Those who make revolution in one generation are often found in later years espousing methods that once again are urged by others to be changed. Syrian leaders whose views had seemed revolutionary in 1920 when the goal was independence, were still what they had been. They expected to lead free Syria in the late 1940s with the same programs they had preached twenty-five years earlier.[2]

With a social system not unlike that of eighteenth century Europe Syria had lived chiefly by trade since Phoenician times. Economic and social power were centered in the cities under merchant, banker, and priest. Feudal landowners paid little heed to political affairs as long as their own prerogatives remained undisturbed. Syrians who perceived a need for radical change concluded, accurately, that change would be impossible until the grip of the mercantile-clerical coalition could be smashed. These were not surviving politicians from the past but revolutionaries of a new, younger breed. Political power was still beyond their reach.

Leaders of the National Bloc reached maturity while Syria was a Turkish province.[3] They came to middle age under European rule. None of them seemed to recognize the tight relationship between political power and the economic apparatus. They were dazzled by the success of parliamentary democracy in the west and did not ask under what conditions such a system could prosper. History suggests that democratic government is in fact the offspring, not the parent, of education and economic betterment. The Bloc proposed in Syria a political system for which its people were not yet equipped.

The Syrian army—undermanned, undertrained, and poorly led as a deliberate policy under a France that feared emergence of a strong native military force—made only a feeble showing against the Zionists in Palestine in 1948–49 and straggled home with nothing but a casualty list. The public laid the blame on the government, which tried to shift responsibility to the generals. The real culprit, of course, was the French imperial system with its lust to remain in power.

Syrian nationalism had always been a civilian movement, with no competent army to nurture it. The political novices at Damascus did not yet realize that armies, which can seldom govern well, nevertheless can and often do determine who shall govern. Colonel Hosni al Zaim seized control on March 20, 1949. His one notable achievement was abolition of the religious courts. He set up a secular judicial system, swept out the old Koranic law, and formed a new legal system based on the Napoleonic code. He dismissed the House of Deputies and took all power into his own hands.

Syria's chief exports were tobacco and grain, and royalist Iraq and Jordan were her principal customers. This relationship forced Al Zaim into cooperation with his customers' political friends in the west. He granted a franchise to the United States-owned Trans-Arabian Pipeline Company (Tapline) for the shipment of Iraqi oil through Syria to the Mediterranean. The previous government had rejected such a deal because the United States was Israel's principal sponsor.

Army men who had put Al Zaim in office resented his collaboration with western powers. He earned popular anger by returning to Lebanon a political refugee, Anton Saadi; the right of political asylum was a cherished Arab tradition. Colonel Sami Hinawi displaced Al Zaim, but neither his coming nor his going mattered much. Hinawi's successor, General Adib al Shishakli, won public support by breaking all ties with Jordan and Iraq to build warmer relations with Egypt. He tried to introduce minor social reforms, but his actions enraged bankers, merchants, and clergy, and he was soon out.

The seesaw record of Syria's disturbed affairs could be read in her relations with other Arab states; she vacillated between lands still in the British grip and those determined to break European control of the Arab world. These changing attitudes reflected the internal contest—the old was still too strong to be eliminated and the new yet too weak to take and hold power. The forces of revolution had not reached agreement on direction or goals, and effective government was impossible. One ruling group yielded to the next and none achieved real mastery.

Christians were a minority, but many of the bourgeoisie adhered to one or another Christian sect and feared submergence in a Muslim-dominated state. They willingly tolerated the French because of a religious tie with the west, and as a group, they were naturally opposed to revolutionary social change.

Pro-Egyptian elements were the most numerous in Syria, but money and power were on the other side. Palestinian refugees came to Syria in tens of thousands, and Palestinian guerillas the results of that upheaval, whichever side might win. The record of Germany between 1933 and 1945 supports this view. Through all the years of Nazi rule an overwhelming majority of Germans repeated the required "Heil Hitler!" on every appropriate occasion. After their crushing defeat they accepted the condemnation of Hitlerism and denied personal participation in or responsibility for the shocking Nazi excesses.

Metternich has said that the revolution begins in the best minds and filters down through the populace. And so it has been. It is probably true that counterrevolution functions in somewhat similar fashion. If Muhammad Naguib in Egypt and Yussef ben Khedda in Algeria had won the initial struggle for political power, the Arab revolution would surely have been delayed, but it seems impossible that revolution could have been prevented. In both countries the conditions that produced revolution *were* intolerable, and it seems equally certain that only massive, drastic social, political, and economic change offered any hope of acceptable improvement. The existing system, which both Naguib and Ben Khedda appeared willing to preserve, had clearly demonstrated its inability to meet the public need. Revolution was both necessary and inevitable.

Radical transformation of society by means of total mobilization of the masses had to be. Algeria achieved it; Egypt had yet to take a step in that direction.

Algeria needed not merely change but complete reconstruction. Independence had wiped away every established agency of government and the European exodus had virtually destroyed the economy. The poverty of the people defied all powers of description.

In March 1963 the government seized all agricultural land abandoned by the fleeing *colons* and the large estens of those who had remained in Algeria. De Gaulle protested that these expropriations violated the Evian-les-Bains agreement. Ben Bella shrugged. "If some argue about texts," he replied, "we argue about morality." Algeria, he said, was merely recovering what had been stolen from her. "Ben Bella is completely indifferent if this violates the Evian accord."

New friction developed when De Gaulle chose the Algerian Sahara in which to detonate France's first atomic bomb. Every free state in that region protested bitterly but vainly. Even then, however, Ben Bella sought friendly relations with France "because," he said, we are realists." France was still the best available market for Algeria's products and the best available source of the help and services that Algeria needed.

The regime outlawed the Communist party but built warm relations with the USSR. "We are not Marxists," Ben Bella said, "but if the Russians did not exist it would be necessary to invent them" as a counterweight to western imperialism. His foreign policy, he declared, would be attuned to the needs of the Arab world. He demanded that monarchy be destroyed and the remnants of European imperialism evicted. No other western power—i.e., the United States—must be permitted to gain a political foothold.

Israel, he asserted, must be destroyed. The United States had sired that state to serve its own imperial purposes and the western world had welcomed it as a dumping ground for its own unwanted Jews. By supporting Israel, Ben Bella insisted, the Christian west was trying to salve its own conscience for the centuries of anti-Jewish oppression which only Christians had practiced. "Israel is a legacy of Hitler and Nazism. Why should the Arabs pay Hitler's debts?"[1]

Morocco's king, who had once supported the Algerian rebels, changed his tune as he watched the advance of the revolution. Like other Arab kings he feared the power and purposes of Egypt's Nasser. In February 1963 he tried to create a federation or league of the Maghreb (northwest Africa) states to offset Egyptian influence in the Arab world. Ben Bella scorned his scheme. "A Casablanca bloc," he argued, "would be a tool in the hands of western imperialists against Arab unity." Common aims and needs, he said, must be the only criteria of inter-Arab relations.

The racist west still believed that only men with fair skins had a right to rule. Few conceded that the darker races could or should govern themselves, and outright defiance of the white western nations by nonwhites created both resentment and wonder. Nasser had been the west's favorite target of abuse; now most westerners promoted Ahmad ben Bella to similar status.

The U.S., proud of its own revolution, attacked the Arab revolution with a special venom. Knowing almost nothing of its origin and justification, most Americans saw that revolution primarily as a barrier to their own nation's ambitions in the Arab world and translated the events of the Arab revolution in terms of the conflict over Palestine and Soviet penetration.

Western governments, however, were not Ben Bella's only foes. Some of his associates in the FLN protested that he moved neither far nor fast enough, and Secretary-General Muhammad Khyder quit his post on this ground. Ben Bella was still a realist; he recognized the limitations that world attitudes and Algeria's own weakness imposed upon him. He was willing to wait when waiting could help him. *Le Monde* of Paris said of him that he had "the patience of a peasant that events have tested and strengthened."

Boumedienne   Access to power is little more than a point of beginning in the revolutionary process. In our time the leaders of revolution have tended to drape their movements in democratic garments and define them in democratic terms because parliamentary democracy is the current vogue. In practice, revolutionary governments rely on autocratic rule because they must. While opposition to the revolution remains strong, the actual use of democratic methods would endanger the whole revolutionary structure.

The popular will remains, nevertheless, extremely important. Participants in the internal power struggle must win public as well as military support and he who gains popular favor has a substantial advantage over his rivals.

To this extent the democratic principle is at work within even the most autocratic revolutionary regime. Victory in this power struggle tends to make the winner a popular hero as well as a recognized leader. Each achievement of the revolution becomes his personal accomplishment, and a personality cult is born.

Ahmed ben Bella like Nasser had something of the demagog in him. They both liked being boss and liked applause. Ben Bella wanted to be *Rais*, as Nasser was called. He saw himself as an important man in world affairs with his name indelibly impressed on Arab history, and the vision encouraged his vanity. While Egypt continued to live under Nasser's personality cult, Algeria preferred to live its ideals. Within the government men who had followed Ben Bella blindly persuaded themselves that to identify the revolution with any one man, whatever his talents, endangered the state and the revolutionary program. The revolution could succeed, they believed, only as the joint enterprise of all its leaders. Vital decisions, they argued, could not be entrusted to any one man's judgment.

Colonel Houari Boumedienne was one of these. Foreign Minister Muhammad Bouteflika was one. Himself austere and sincere, Boumedienne began to resent Ben Bella's elevation almost to godhead. Native ability, intuitive political skill, and a dominant personality had made him a hero at home, and whatever he did seemed to brighten his luster. At home and abroad he had become Algeria.

On June 19, 1965, Boumedienne took Ben Bella into custody in the name of a new Revolutionary Command.

This laying of hands on the national idol roused a popular storm. Day after day tens of thousands demonstrated in city streets demanding Ben Bella's release. These outbursts ran on for a fortnight, and Boumedienne made no attempt to suppress them. The army, under his command, did nothing. Because there was no brutal repression of the protests, little or no violence developed. Gradually the demonstrations petered out.

Boumedienne remained true to his faith in collective leadership. He avoided the publicity and self-seeking that Ben Bella
had courted. His was the driving voice in the Revolutionary
Command, but in appearance, at least, the revolution became
the common enterprise he had said it must be. Like Nasser he
saw independence as freedom not only from foreign military
occupation but from endemic social problems. Boumedienne
stuck to that priority while Nasser's foolhardy dreams of gran-
deur led him from that path.

Cautiously, western powers accepted the change, not because
they trusted Boumedienne but because they had feared his predecessor. Even within Algeria Boumedienne was less well known
than any other revolutionary leader. His earlier life was a
mystery. Of only this were men sure: he was a devout Muslim
dedicated to his country, with no known vices or ambitions.

The economic situation was still desperate. War had laid
waste once productive farms. French troops trying to flush
guerillas from their hiding places had burned hundreds of thousands of valuable forest acres. French soldiers had slaughtered
most of Algeria's livestock or left the animals to starve in
burned-out areas that provided no forage.

Algeria had almost nobody qualified by education, training,
and experience to run factories or manage large scale trade.
This shortage of needed manpower was part of the heritage
left by France. At least a third of the people had no jobs. Men,
women, and children subsisted on aid from France, the United
States, Great Britain, Russia, and China in the form of food,
shelter, medical help, and some materials for reconstruction of
devastated areas.

Petroleum offered the one bright spot in Algeria's future. A
national petroleum syndicate, Sonatrach, gave the government
effective control of this resource. Sonatrach did not take possession of the oil fields but assigned concessions, delineated the
areas within which concessionnaires might operate, dictated
what share of the domestic market each might serve at what

prices, and regulated the royalties each must pay. Sonatrach also built a pipeline to the coast and fixed transit fees. The discovery of rich natural gas deposits and the demand for gas in Europe increased the prospect of early prosperity.

The Evian accord gave a substantial price advantage in Algeria's domestic market to the French. In 1966 some United States firms demanded equal treatment, and Washington used its store of surplus foodstuffs to try to force compliance. Boumedienne refused to yield. The companies protested. Sonatrach revoked the charter of El Paso Natural Gas and nationalized some marketing firms. The American demands and United States threats were quickly dropped.

War 1967   When Israel attacked four Arab states in 1967, Algeria sent troops to join the struggle, but the United Nations cease-fire order had been issued and accepted before they reached the scene of the fighting. Algeria, Iraq, and Syria urged all Arab nations to renew the conflict, but neither Hussein nor Nasser had any desire for more fighting just then. Nasser began to talk vaguely of a political rather than a military settlement. Boumedienne, fearing that a sellout was about to be attempted, refused to join the Arab summit meeting at Khartum in August.

Despite 132 years of occupation and oppression, Algeria maintained good relations with France, as De Gaulle had believed she would. The two countries needed each other. Each had goods and products that the other required. Other western powers feared the revolutionary character of the Algerian government, but France took the sensible position that Algeria's choice of a politico-economic system was her own affair. Permanently out of the empire business themselves, the French saw no reason to oppose the development of revolution and Arab nationalism in Algeria.

17: MOROCCO

A king as nationalist?

IF REVOLUTION be no more than the transfer of power, Morocco has not known revolution. The people were Arabs and Berbers, almost all Muslims. The two groups had lived almost entirely apart from each other since the Arab conquest. Turkey claimed sovereignty over Morocco after the fifteenth century but never had much power there. The native sultan held absolute power. Because an organized clergy is often the mainstay of despotism, the Islamic priesthood was far more powerful here than ever it had been in Algeria. France claimed a protectorate over most of the country in 1912.

Moroccans were farmers, either growing fruits and grain or breeding livestock. Pasture was excellent. France was not in Morocco long enough to build a large European population; nevertheless, by 1939 almost all vineyards and citrus groves were owned by Frenchmen or the Roman Catholic church, the largest single landholder. Industry and commerce were largely in French hands.

Sheiks and regional pashas still dominated the Berbers, but among the Arabs tribalism had long since broken down. Farmers took no interest in political affairs and relatively few Moroccans faced the squalid hopelessness of urban life, but a strong spirit of nationalism, fostered by Sultan Muhammad V, developed rapidly as French administrators restricted the royal authority and fixed French rule on every phase of Moroccan

163

life. A new nationalist party called Istiqlal came into being in January 1943. The name means freedom or independence.

Abd el Krim   Muhammad V was only one among many Moroccans who had dreamed of and planned for national freedom. When in 1912 France proclaimed her protectorate over Morocco, Spain, which had long held Ceuta on the Strait of Gibraltar and the nearby port of Melilla, protested. In the resulting deal the Spanish got a protectorate over what was called the northern zone of the country.

Sheik Muhammad ben Abd el Krim took part in one of the first Moroccan attacks against the Spaniards, who had just occupied the holy city of Chechaoueg. He saw his father and many of his family slaughtered by Spanish soldiers. Muhammad himself was captured and spent eleven months in prison in Spain.

In 1921 he gathered four hundred men from his El Khattaba tribe and swept down in a furious cavalry charge against a strong Spanish outpost. Most of the Spaniards there died. Abd el Krim's success rallied other tribes to his side, and they fell on a Spanish army of twenty-one thousand men near Melilla. Other raids and battles followed and the Moroccan chieftain matched wits and skills with a youthful Spanish Colonel named Francisco Franco, who was later to fasten his iron grip on Spain.

Abd el Krim set up a Republic of the Riff and turned his eyes on the part of Morocco that France ruled. In a savage battle north of Fez he smashed the first army the French sent against him. France and Spain combined forces to field another force of some 160 thousand men, all of them colonial troops from their African possessions. Krim's army had grown, too, as tribesmen from all of Morocco put themselves under his command, but the Franco-Spanish army outnumbered him four to one. The Europeans drove him back from some of the areas he had seized, but they could not capture him. Then, in

1926, bribery and treachery began to diminish his army and he surrendered rather than lead his still loyal followers to destruction.

France sent him and his entourage into exile on the Indian Ocean island of Reunion, and he lived there twenty-one years. Still an ardent Moroccan nationalist, he watched the rise of Franco to power in Spain and the restoration of the French colonial empire after World War II.

In 1947 the French granted permission for Muhammad ben Abd el Krim to live in a villa near Cannes and put him aboard ship for the voyage to a new home. At Port Said he slipped ashore and found in Egypt both a refuge and a welcome. His name was still a legend and a battle cry in the Maghreb. On occasion he thundered against those Arabs still disposed to collaborate with European imperialists, and on occasion he threatened to return to Morocco to lead another holy war if his own countrymen faltered in their struggle for independence.

In February 1963 Muhammad ben Abd el Krim died, his name indelibly written on the history not only of Morocco but of the whole Arab battle for freedom from foreign colonization.

Fight for Freedom   United States troops landed in Morocco in November 1942 to help Britain against the Germans in north Africa. Morocco became an American base. Moroccan nationalists supposed that the United States was still an apostle of the rights of men and nations. With American support, they believed, Morocco could soon be free again. But the United States had abandoned its historic role as the preacher and leader of enslaved men's right to independence. Now the goal of the United States in the Arab world was continuing western control of that region with its riches and its strategic geographic position. The France of Charles de Gaulle assumed political rule in Morocco and the situation was just about what it had been in 1939. Sultan Muhammad V refused to be a French puppet. Speaking at Tangier in April 1947 he demanded his state's independence. France set new restrictions on his royal power, and in the process gave Morocco what she had not had since Krim's surrender, a new hero and a shining new national symbol.

France established a French Union modeled after the British Commonwealth of Nations and asked Morocco to join it. Muhammad V responded with a formal demand for total freedom. When Paris rejected his claim, violent demonstrations erupted at Casablanca, Marrakech, and Meknes. The French fired every suspected nationalist who held a public job and ordered the sultan to discharge every Istiqlal sympathizer from the royal secretariat. He ignored their command.

Tami al Glaoui   Morocco was a protectorate, not a colony. Nominally Sultan Muhammad V ruled the country, and every law, every decree, required his signature to make it valid, even though in fact they were all French commands. The sultan outwitted France for a time by refusing to sign anything and paralyzed the civil administration. Very soon the French turned to Tami al Glaoui for help.

Al Glaoui was a Berber chief, strongest and most powerful man among the Berbers. Long before the Arabs came to Morocco, his family had exercised despotic authority. No Glaoui had ever forgiven the Arabs for their conquest or acknowledged their authority. The ancient feud still rankled. Indeed, Tami al Glaoui and his brother Si Mahani had helped France achieve her protectorate in order to set a brake on Arab power. Now, when the French invited him to assume the power to sign laws and decrees, he went along with them. When, however, they presented a law banning Istiqlal for his signature, he backed away. That decree, he knew, would stir a popular storm that not even a Glaoui could survive.

Al Glaoui's collaboration with the French had robbed the sultan of his best weapon. Nothing seemed to be left but a resort to civil war. Al Glaoui boasted that he could send enough armed Berbers against Muhammad V to drive him off his throne. The sultan hedged a little and offered to settle with France for internal autonomy and an all-Moroccan government.

France refused, and went to Al Glaoui again. As pasha of Marrakech he summoned a convocation of Berber leaders who promptly demanded Muhammad's abdication. The sultan shrugged them off. In August 1953 the French took him into custody and sent him off to exile on the Indian Ocean island of Reunion. On his throne they set his cousin Moulay Muhammad ben Arifa, a weak and obscure nonentity. Muhammad V's arrest lighted fires of rebellion wherever Arabs were.

Fighting another colonial war was beyond French capacity. In Indochina French troops had just absorbed an ignominious defeat. Algerian rebels had gone to war to win their freedom. In the cities of Tunisia angry men were demonstrating and rioting. Paris officials recognized that the sultan's dethronement had been a blunder and offered him back his job.

Free Morocco   Muhammad in his island exile received their offer cooly. Life on Reunion, he believed, was better than nominal kingship as a prisoner of French imperialism. He would return only as the unfettered monarch of Morocco. France yielded. Her other colonial problems had forced her hand. She promised not only to abolish her protectorate but to persuade the Spanish to get out of the zone they held.

Muhammad V abandoned the title of sultan and began to call himself king. Ben Arifa faded into oblivion from which he had sprung. Tami al Glaoui, that once arrogant pasha of Marrakech, groveled on his belly before his monarch with a plea for pardon and the pledge of allegiance that no other Glaoui had given. The king went home a greater national hero than he had ever been.

The revolutionary ferment that was spreading through the

Arab world had not yet begun to trouble Morocco. Since the days of the Arab empire her economic contacts had been almost wholly with the west. She joined the Arab League, but the king neither sought nor welcomed Arab ties beyond the Maghreb region of north Africa.

During the second world war the United States had set up military bases in Morocco with Free French permission. After that war the United States kept them, chiefly as relay stations for direct contact with such places as Saudi Arabia. The fees that Washington paid, along with the wages of native workers and the money spent for local supplies and services, constituted a very substantial item in the national economy.

It is not always easy to remember that national pride may demand some return more important than money. The foreigners in Morocco were now Americans instead of Frenchmen, but they remained foreigners. As the United States role in the Arab world grew more blatant a burgeoning sense of Moroccan kinship with other Arabs produced a demand that the United States abandon its local bases.

King Muhammad needed United States money, but he needed public approval even more. The bases, he argued, were held under an agreement with a European power that had neither legal nor moral right to barter away Moroccan territory. Washington yielded. The rapid development of long range aircraft had made the Moroccan fields less important as way stations to the Arabian peninsula and Iran. Increasing Arab hostility in many lands made it especially desirable to preserve cordial relations with countries like Morocco.

Ben Barka   Muhammad V died in February 1962. His son and heir, Hassan II, had built a reputation as a playboy whose chief interests were best served by fast horses and complaisant women. Few anywhere had any confidence in his capacities as a ruler. Until his accession revolutionaries in Morocco had bided their time, but now they believed that their hour had struck. They formed a political party, the Union of Popular Forces, and demanded an end to monarchy.

Hassan proved himself an abler, more ruthless ruler than anyone had thought he could be. He established a written constitution designed to affirm his own authority. He named himself premier and supreme military commander, and created a political party with the unwieldy (in English) name, Front for the Preservation of Constitutional Institutions. He called elections for May, 1964 to choose a national consultative assembly (its name betrayed its powerlessness) and promised municipal elections at a later date. The municipal polling never took place. In May his party won barely half the assembly seats. Every member of his cabinet was a candidate for one of those seats, but only one of them survived the balloting.

Hassan ignored the new assembly and ruled by decree. Security forces tracked down every leader they could find among the members of the Union of Popular Forces and jailed them, but one important man escaped. Mehdi ben Barka fled safely to Switzerland.

Ben Barka had been a mathematics teacher before he turned to politics. (As a boy King Hassan had been one of his pupils.) He became an ardent advocate of Arab nationalism and the revolution and its principal Moroccan leader. Agents of General Muhammad Oufkir, Hassan's security chief, lured him out of his Swiss refuge to Paris to meet with other Moroccan revolutionaries. Men in French uniforms seized him outside a Left Bank cafe at noon, and no one but his captors ever saw him again.[1]

Ben Barka's disappearance stirred a political storm in France. In January 1966 President De Gaulle admitted that his own secret police had kidnapped the man and turned him over to Oufkir's agents. The available evidence indicated that Oufkir himself had come to France secretly and watched while Ben

Barka was killed by torture. De Gaulle issued an international warrant charging Oufkir with murder; every member state of Interpol, the worldwide police organization, was obligated to arrest the Moroccan security chief if he entered its territory.

Some shady French characters were brought to trial, but abruptly the case was dropped when Oufkir's deputy commander appeared in the French court and offered to stand trial for his part in the Ben Barka affair. Rumor reported that De Gaulle's good friend and interior minister, Roget Frey, was personally involved in the case and that public airing of his role would split the government and the country wide open. No other plausible explanation was ever offered to justify the sudden abandonment of the prosecution.

Morocco and the Revolution[2]   Hassan pulled farther away from the rest of the Arab world and toward closer alignment with the west. He tried vainly for membership in the European Common Market and invited United States investment in Morocco. In 1967, when every other Arab state denounced the Israeli attack upon Egypt, Jordan, and Syria, he held his silence.

Reports seeped from Hassan's jails that his police were using physical and mental torture to learn the names of still uncaught revolutionaries. Some, it was known, had died in the course of their questioning, but secrecy shrouded the fate of all men charged with plotting against the king.

In March 1965 a student demonstration at Casablanca blossomed into riots there and elsewhere. The army quelled the disorders and the government said nine persons had died. Western observers placed the toll nearer four hundred. At Paris two hundred Moroccan students invaded their country's embassy and defiled pictures of Hassan.

Unrest and disorder broke out sporadically. Hundreds of students and others were picked up and herded into Hassan's jails. Then on Saturday, July 17, 1971, armed men from a camp outside Rabat broke into the palace courtyard where the king was celebrating his forty-second birthday. Hassan escaped, but generals and other high army officers, the Belgian ambassador, and dozens of other guests died. Many more were wounded.

The coup was led by General Muhammad Medbouh, Hassan's friend and commander of the household guard, who was himself killed during the shooting. The arrival of loyal troops squelched the coup, but the mere fact that it had been attempted illustrated the dangers that faced the king and his dynasty.

The country was filled with unrest and resentment. Per capita annual income, sixty dollars in 1960, had risen little if at all since then. The population had grown from nine to thirteen million in ten years, but food production had increased only five percent, providing less food for each mouth than before Morocco won her independence. Only aid from the United States kept the country on its feet.

Another problem troubled many people. It had been generally believed that United States military forces had left Morocco years earlier, but in fact American service personnel still occupied two of the bases. One of these was at Kenitra, the former Port Lyautey, where the U.S. Navy continued to maintain a large communications base for NATO and for the Sixth Fleet in the Mediterranean.

A last minute escape from plans to assassinate him on his birthday was Hassan's last hurrah. Bribery in government and corruption in high circles were becoming too obvious to be concealed. Hassan was squandering as extravagantly as when he was a playboy prince in Paris. His unpopularity was growing as fast as his government was faltering. Radical changes were needed, and his effort to ferret out some corrupt members of the government in November 1971 were regarded as tokenism. But can a king be a radical? The time for pious nationalistic feelings was passing. The revolution was on the move. That the king knew it only too well was evident; word leaked out that one of his many residences outside the country, at Senlis, France, (near Paris) was being refurbished feverishly.[3] On

January 31, 1972, over one thousand, mostly military personnel, were brought to trial on various charges of attempt against the king and the established government.

MAURITANIA

Some countries on the rim of the Arab world, although not themselves wholly Arab, are so intimately associated with and influenced by Arab culture and history that without a knowledge of their record and their attitudes no full understanding of the Arab world is possible.

One such is Mauritania, on the Atlantic coast of Africa south of Morocco. In the east it has a common frontier with Algeria. Southward it reaches the Senegal River. The southern tribes are African blacks. The people of the northern region are wholly or largely Arab and Berber, speaking Arabic. Islam is the state religion; indeed, the state calls itself the Islamic Republic of Mauritania.

Mauritania—or Chenguit as it was formerly known—has long been a natural cultural and commercial bridge between the blacks of central Africa and the Arabs and Berbers. The Maributun (Almovarid) dynasty established that bridge more than nine hundred years ago at the zenith of the Arab empire. Muslim missionaries had been preaching Islam to the peoples of Chenguit three centuries earlier.

Several historians confirm the early union of Morocco and Chenguit. The Arab historian Ahmad ibn al Alim wrote that "the inhabitants of Chenguit and Morocco have always considered the country to be part of the Maghreb." The German Karl Brockelmann says that Almovarid authority ran from Africa's north coast to the Senegal.

Chenguiti emirs traditionally accepted investiture at the hands of Moroccan sultans and turned to them for help when help was needed. In 1902 the French invaded Chenguit from Senegal. The emirs called upon Sultan Abdul Aziz, and he sent an army under his uncle Moulay Idris. Together the Moroccans and Chenguitis held the invaders at bay for two years.

Then France bombarded Casablanca and some other ports and demanded Moulay's recall. Abdul Aziz brought him home, but the tribes kept up their resistance long after France proclaimed Chenguit a colony in 1920 and changed its name to Mauritania. The French did not establish full military control until 1934. In 1946 France took Mauritania into its abortive French Union.

Morocco had never abandoned its claim to that region, and for years this insistence on Moroccan sovereignty created constant friction with the rulers of the new state, jealous of the power and authority they had gained. In 1958 a delegation of Mauritanian leaders from the Arab-Berber north visited Rabat to renew their pledge of fealty to the sultan. In 1960 President De Gaulle proclaimed Mauritania an independent, sovereign state.

In 1969 King Hassan of Morocco formally renounced his claims in Mauritania and the climate of ill will faded. In world affairs Mauritania sided always with the Arab states in any confrontation with the imperial western powers, and its territory, straddling the line between the Arab Maghreb and the black countries of central Africa, continued to provide a pathway for the spread of Arab culture and Arab trade into the farther reaches of the African continent.

18: TUNISIA AND HABIB BOURGUIBA

A nation's tale
and a personal story

THROUGH MORE than a generation the history of Tunisia was the life story of one man, Habib Bourguiba. In other Arab lands leaders rose and fell or faded or passed away, but in Tunisia one man dominated the struggle for independence and the first years of the country's independence.

At the Congress of Berlin in 1878 Britain and France made a secret deal: Paris would recognize British primacy on the island of Cyprus and London would acknowledge the demand of Paris for a free hand in Tunisia. In 1881 a French army crossed into that state from Algeria on the pretense that the soldiers were pursuing Algerian rebels. In 1883 the reigning bey signed a treaty that conceded a French protectorate over his realm.

Habib Bourguiba was born in 1903. His family was prosperous and gave him a good education. He earned degrees in law and political science, and in 1930 he established a nationalist newspaper. In 1934 he became secretary general of a new nationalist party, Destour. The French banned Destour and jailed Bourguiba. Leon Blum freed him in 1936 but the next French government sent him to prison again.

174

The Germans released him in 1940, hoping to use him to promote the Nazi cause in the Arab world, but their creed revolted him. Their vile anti-Jewish campaign nauseated this Arab whose ancestors had lived in harmony with Jews for thirteen centuries. The Germans let him go home, confident that if he would not serve them, at least he would do nothing to aid the French. After the war he appealed to De Gaulle to set Tunisia free, but the De Gaulle of 1945 was the same imperialist who denied independence to Syria, Lebanon, and Indochina.

Depression and war had wrecked the Tunisian economy, and hardship pressed most heavily upon the native population. Since 1881, here as in Algeria, France had settled tens of thousands of her own people on the land. Most valuable farmland belonged to Frenchmen and Catholic interests.

Hunger and joblessness exacerbated the hatred of colonialism. Resentment of the foreign presence bred a new Tunisian nationalism. Habib Bourguiba fanned these sentiments, and on April of 1945 De Gaulle ordered him imprisoned again. This time, however, he evaded capture. He preached Tunisia's cause in Arab countries, Europe, and the Americas, finding time now and then to slip back into his own land to stir new unrest.

The man made himself a hero to every native Tunisian. Many of them imagined that foreign control was the cause of all their woes. Independence, they believed, would almost automatically solve their problems. The middle and upper classes trusted Bourguiba because he was one of their own. Men at the base of the social heap followed him because he offered them hope.

France tried to counter the new nationalism with an all-native cabinet as a front for the colonial administration, but no known and respected nationalist could be coaxed into it. In September 1949 Paris let Bourguiba return. In April 1950 he abandoned his demand for independence and offered to settle for autonomy. Nothing on public record explains this sudden change. In any event, France granted much of what he asked and many Tunisian nationalists joined Bourguiba in an all-native government from which all French advisers had been withdrawn.

Independence   Autonomy neither deceived nor satisfied most politically aware Tunisians. France was still boss, and some of Bourguiba's strongest supporters turned from him. He changed direction again and insisted upon independence. The remark attributed to Mahatma Ghandi might as well have been his; "There go my people. I must catch up with them, for I am their leader."

Tunisia asked the United Nations to order French withdrawal, but the United Nations was then a spokesman for the west. Tunisia, Paris insisted, was a French internal problem outside United Nations jurisdiction. Great Britain and the United States agreed. The French clamped Habib Bourguiba into jail again.

Public meetings demanded his release. Demonstrations developed, and out of the demonstrations grew riots. In the mountain regions revolt appeared. French troops fought guerillas whom they could not defeat and often could not find. The world had forgotten that Tunisia was nominally still a monarchy until in July 1954 Premier Mendes-France at Paris instructed the bey to proclaim complete autonomy and name a new government.

Some guerillas laid down their arms, but others fought on. They wanted freedom, not autonomy which would leave French troops in occupation and Frenchmen controlling the economy.

In Algeria the FLN kept a large French army tied down. In Morocco a stubborn sultan supported by guerillas had forced France to grant full freedom. On March 20, 1956, Paris made Tunisia independent. Habib Bourguiba set up a free Tunisian government.

Between Two Worlds[1]   Tunisia, with Morocco, was tied economically to the west, and the relatively simple transition from protectorate to sovereignty did not disturb this relationship.

The nation joined the League of Arab States but its voice there was usually a western, not an Arab voice. A widening gulf yawned between Tunisia and most Arab countries.

Nationalism in the Arab world had long been a purely local patriotism that stopped at national frontiers. Now, however, with Egypt and Nasser pointing the way, the nationalist idea began to embrace all Arabs everywhere. The leaders of Arab nationalism were also the leaders of the Arab revolution. Their drive for Arab unity demanded an end to all Arab dependence upon and collaboration with the western imperial powers. Where such bonds remained, the Arab nationalists insisted, only revolution could sunder them. Thus the division of the Arab world into two camps developed. Those aligned with the west opposed both Arab nationalism and the revolution and carried their opposition into Arab League councils.

Bourguiba no more favored Arab nationalism and revolution than did the king of Morocco. These two, with the kings of Saudi Arabia, Jordan, and Libya and the Persian Gulf sheiks, sailed together in a leaky, reactionary vessel that seemed almost certain to founder some day. Of these, however, only Habib Bourguiba and Hassan II refused to join a front against Israel.

Bourguiba's attitude toward Israel has already been mentioned. His American-sponsored attempt to win Arab recognition of the Zionist state and the dispersion of the Palestinians from the neighborhood of Israel's borders made him at the time a pariah in most of the Arab world.[2]

Those Tunisian nationalists loyal to Bourguiba followed the parochial concept of nationalism that other Arabs had given up. Other men rejected Bourguiba and his ideas because he was purposely leading the state out of the common Arab world. Salah ibn Yussef, long his ardent supporter, denounced him as a lackey of the west. Bourguiba charged Ibn Yussef with treason, but he fled to Cairo. There he was mysteriously murdered.

Tunisia and the Revolution   The Tunisian economy was woefully weak, and independence had done nothing to improve it.

Only massive outside help made survival possible. His middle class background and Tunisia's long dependence on western markets turned Bourguiba to the west for the aid he needed. Conditions got a little better, but the basic problems remained.

Chief among these was French economic control. Foreigners dominated business and industry. Foreigners, including the Roman church, controlled all the best agricultural land. Bourguiba ignored popular discontent with his pro-westernism as long as he dared, but the time came when bitter demonstrations could no longer be shrugged aside. Per capita annual income was only $150. Most of the wealth the country produced was being drained off into foreign banks and corporation treasuries. Social progress was almost nil. By contrast the social and economic reforms going forward in the revolutionary Arab states provided fuel for a growing hostility to Bourguiba and his lack of any clear program of progress.

In May 1965 Bourguiba abruptly nationalized all foreign-owned land, including the vast estates of the Catholic church.[3] France protested and cut off, temporarily, the economic aid she had been providing. Expropriation made every Catholic (and almost exclusively French or Italian) parish a hotbed of resistance. The government thereupon seized all church buildings and forbade Catholic religious services without special permits except in Tunis, Sousa, and Bizerta. Bourguiba jailed every protesting landlord. "If," he said, "the principles of Karl Marx are proved true, according to which cooperation with the capitalists is impossible, then we shall adopt them."[4]

The constant threat of the Arab revolution and the harsh conditions of Tunisian life appeared to be driving the man much farther left than he cared to go, but he kept his country inside the western orbit. The United States tended to tolerate his seizure of agricultural land because no Americans were hurt by it and other American investments in Tunisia were growing. Besides, the man was still useful as an opponent of the Arab revolution.

of Sheba remained the principal roads. There were no public schools and no telephones, no hospitals, not one modern town. In all the eleven centuries that had passed while Muhammad al Badr's family reigned at Sana'a life in the north had changed almost not at all. Tribal warriors skilled in ancient ways of battle gave an excellent account of themselves in warfare against the republicans, but they seldom dared to venture into situations where republican mobility and firepower put them at a disadvantage.

1967 The revolution in Yemen produced just such an internal struggle for power as those in Egypt and Algeria. Men intent on revolutionary change encountered opposition from others who, willing though they were to abolish a monarchy, had no stomach for the fundamental revision of the social and economic conditions under which Yemeni Arabs lived.

President Nasser, in control of the Egyptian army he had sent to Yemen, exercised almost a veto over the revolutionary program in the beginning, and the United States took advantage of this fact to impose pressure on the republic by putting pressure on Egypt. In 1964 Nasser agreed to a deal with King Faisal of Saudi Arabia over Al Sallal's protests, and only because Washington used America's store of surplus foodstuffs (which Egypt still needed) as a club over his head.

Some of those who supported Colonel Al Sallal wanted in Yemen (as Naguib had sought in Egypt) little more than gradual, painless reform, and in late 1965 these advocates of mild reform, led by a conservative army man, Major General Hassan al Amiri, gained the upper hand for a time. Nine months later in August 1966 revolutionaries won control at Sana'a again. Al Sallal returned. He ordered Major General Abdul Rahman Iriani, the strong man of Al Sallal's domestic foes, into exile in Egypt, where Nasser's police kept him under surveillance. The process of change in Yemen picked up momentum again.

The growing Arab-Israeli conflict in May 1967 played an

important part in the progress of the Yemeni revolution even
though Yemen was never directly involved in that confrontation. When Syria called upon Egypt for help, Nasser was seriously handicapped by the fact that a large part of his army—
including many of his best troops—were tied down in Yemen.
He had to pull some of them out for deployment in Sinai.

When the Suez Canal was closed in June 1967, the cessation
of traffic through the waterway shut off a substantial portion of
Egypt's income. Oil had been found in Sinai and now the
Israelis had that. There was no available source of compensatory
help except the wealthy petroleum-producing states of Libya,
Kuwait, and Saudi Arabia. Just as surely as the United States
since 1945 had been demanding political concessions in return
for the aid it gave weaker countries, now the three Arab monarchs imposed conditions and Nasser was forced to enter a new
deal on Yemen. What the Yemeni republic wanted or needed
was no longer of any special importance; Nasser was now look-
ing out for his own immediate interest. As part of the agreement
with King Faisal, Nasser promised to remove from Yemen all
the soldiers still there, leaving the republicans to fight their own
battles thereafter. This 1967 deal in other respects was much
like the one that had failed in 1964, with the additional pro-
provision that Sudan, Morocco, and Iraq would supervise the
carrying out of its terms.[5]

Abdullah al Sallal refused even to consider the terms that
Nasser had accepted. Yemen, he insisted, could not permit any
other state to compromise the revolution. His comment was
ironically reminiscent of the sort of thing that other Arab states
had been saying when the United States tried to interfere with
their revolutionary programs—but this time the rebuke was
being leveled at the man and the country who had initiated
revolution in the Arab world. Nasser's leadership of the Arab
nation and the Arab revolution sustained a severe blow. He
stood revealed as a man less interested in the Arab national
revolution than in his own political survival.

From Sana'a Abdullah al Sallal set off on a journey to Moscow. The Soviet Union was preparing to celebrate the fiftieth anniversary of its founding, and this event provided a plausible reason for the Yemeni leader's trip. His principal reason, however, appears to have been to seek more Soviet help for his struggle against the Yemeni royalists.

He got only as far as Baghdad in Iraq. On Sunday, November 5, 1967, General Abdul Rahman Iriani, who had been in exile at Cairo, and Moshen al Awni, who had once been Al Sallal's minister of foreign affairs, seized control of the Sana'a government with help from conservative senior army men whom the republicans had permitted to keep their posts. President Nasser —unhappy with Al Sallal's rejection of his deal with Faisal and with the blow his prestige had taken as a consequence—had released Iriani on October 27 and sent him secretly into Yemen for just this purpose. In the Arab world, as elsewhere, big states were not above trying to manage the affairs of weaker states for their own selfish reasons.

Iriani managed to establish a truce of sorts with the sheiks supporting Imam Muhammad al Badr. His aim appears to have been to persuade them to accept the fact of revolution in the south by promising that it would not be extended into their territories. The royalists, under Saudi Arabian prodding, broke the truce almost while they were agreeing to it. In December they moved an army through Saudi Arabia to encircle the republican capital at Sana'a. In that force were many of the mercenaries whom Faisal had recruited and paid for service in Yemen. The assault failed, and the fighting subsided once more.

Within the republic the revolution went on. Omelets are not easily unscrambled, and the revolution had advanced too far ever to be turned back.

For centuries despots and zealots had been distorting and abusing the precepts of Islamic law to serve their own ends, and a very substantial element of the clergy had accommodated itself to this fact. The republic had abolished Koranic law as the basis of its legal system and substituted a secular system based on the Napoleonic code. Human slavery, practiced under the imams although never admitted, was done away with. Minor miscreants could no longer be hanged at a ruler's whim nor an adulteress be stoned to death. A man could have but one wife. Concubinage was forbidden. Neither could a family patriarch sell his daughter into marriage or whoredom. The Yemeni revolution was in high gear.

Most women discarded the veil of purdah. Many worked now at money wages for the first time. Foreign trade was a government monopoly. This phase of the revolution was more easily accomplished in Yemen than in Egypt and Algeria because the merchant class had always been small and because the economy had never been under foreign control. No foreign state had any pretext now to intervene to protect its citizens' investments.

King Faisal of Saudi Arabia and his predecessor Saud had been the Yemeni republic's bitterest foes and the chief protectors of the deposed imam, Muhammad al Badr. Now Faisal recognized that the Arab revolution had scored another success, this time at his own doorstep. He also realized that successful opposition to the Yemeni republic was beyond his capacities, and in 1970 he recognized the revolutionary government at Sana'a.

Western observers seemed firmly convinced that President Gamal Abdul Nassar of Egypt had taken his prestige and his troops into Yemen with a determination to establish Egyptian hegemony there and to set up a base within each of the rich oil resources of the Persian Gulf sheikdoms. Speculations were that Nasser's real goals were oil-rich Kuwait, the emirates, and eventually Saudi Arabia. These prospects were bolstered by as many as fifty thousand Egyptian troops plus part of the air force in Yemen. Egyptian generals appeared to be in charge of Yemeni military operations in the civil war, and advisors were quite apparent in the civilian branch of government.

The western assumptions were plausible enough and there may well have been some truth in them, but calmer judgment suggests that other considerations may have provided the basis for Nasser's determined effort to save the infant Yemeni republic from collapse.

Yemen had joined the Arab revolution of which Gamal Abdul Nasser was hailed as its acknowledged leader. Yemen was also the first Arab state in which opposition from other Arabs seemed at one time likely to defeat the revolution and set it back for nobody knew how many years. Nasser's ego, his most cherished plans, and his own prestige as leader of the Arab world were at stake. They probably could not easily have survived a Yemeni failure—particularly at the hands of the Saudi Arabian kingdom, the Arab world's richest and strongest foe of revolution and of Nasser. Oddly enough his intervention did little to endear him the Yemeni leadership, and the presence of Egyptian troops in a combat role generated resentment among the people. Both reactions were to be short lived, and in due time his decisive intervention which saved the Yemeni republic accelerated the advance of the Arab revolution in that part of the world by decades.

22: SAUDI ARABIA AND IBN SAUD
The oil and desert kingdom

As THE RECENT history of Tunisia was primarily the story of Habib Bourguiba, so the history of Saudi Arabia, from its founding until his death, was the biography of Abdul Aziz ibn Saud.

Western nations seeking Arab empires long ignored the central regions of the Arabian peninsula. It appeared to be no more than a barren wasteland sparsely populated by warring Arab tribes. Neither the land nor anything within it seemed worth the money and blood they would have had to spend to acquire it.

Interior Arabia was indeed the homeland of feuding tribesmen. The Hashimi clan held Hejaz with the holy cities of Medina and Mecca in the west. The Rashidi family ruled Hasa and Djebel Shamar. The Saudi emirs controlled Nejd from their capital at Riyadh. In 1891 Ibn Rashid captured Riyadh and the Saudis fled to Kuwait. Ten years later Abdul Aziz ibn Saud set out with a small, loyal band to regain his heritage. He was twenty-one years old. Outside Riyadh he and fifteen of his men hid in a cemetery until nightfall, slipped into the city, and seized the governor's palace. There Abdul Aziz proclaimed himself emir of Nejd.

For generations the Turks had preserved their overlordship

in central Arabia by playing one ruler off against another. Now
they backed Ibn Rashid against Ibn Saud, and lost. Before 1914
Abdul Aziz ibn Saud ruled not only Nejd but all of Ibn Rashid's
domain as well.

The Wahabis   In the eighteenth century a Muslim mullah,
Muhammad Abdul Wahab, founded a puritanical sect still
known by his name. His goal was the restoration of a rigid
Islamic theocracy through all Arabia, but his rules were too
harsh for most tribal chiefs' liking and they chased him beyond
their domains. He found a haven at Riyadh with the emir of
Nejd. Abdul Aziz, when he came to power, established a Wahabi
ikhwan—brotherhood—and sent its members through his newly
won territories on a mission both spiritual and political. Their
labors bore fruit. With their help Ibn Saud's authority was
secure.

Even in those early days Ibn Saud appears to have planned
to make himself sole king of Arabia. He drove to the Persian
Gulf and encountered the British rulers of the Gulf sheikdoms.
In 1914 they tried to enlist him in their war against the Turks,
but Ibn Saud did not succumb to their pleas. He knew enough
Arab history to see the risks in such a course and did not propose to let any western power get a foothold inside his realm.
He did, however, promise not to support Britian's enemies when
she recognized him as emir of Nejd and Hasa and pledged a
modest annual subsidy.

Britain, turned down by Ibn Saud, offered the same bait to
Sherif Hussein ibn Hashim of Hejaz, and sweetened the offer
with a promise to make Hussein king of an independent Arab
nation when the war had been won. As Satan is said to have
shown Jesus of Nazareth all the kingdoms of earth, now Britain
turned Hussein's ambitious gaze on Lebanon, Syria, Palestine,
and most of the Arabian peninsula. All he got out of the deal
was the city of Khurma, and when he occupied Khurma, Ibn
Saud used his presence there as a pretext to destroy him.

Khurma straddled the caravan route from Riyadh to Mecca. A Saudi army attacked the Hashimites at Zuraba and pushed forward to the frontier of Transjordan. In 1924 Ibn Saud moved on Mecca. Hussein abdicated. His son Ali lost all of Hejaz and Ibn Saud added that region to his territory. He proclaimed a new Kingdom of Saudi Arabia (literally, the Saudis' Arabia) with himself as its king.

Oil   Ibn Saud's kingdom was large and his power absolute. Every life in it was his to guard or to end. Slavery was a way of life. Medieval Islamic law in its harshest form was the national code. There were no schools. Orthodox Islam was the only religious faith permitted. The social structure was that of ancient Arab tribalism and most of the tribesmen were nomads. The Wahabi clergy wielded more authority than the clergy in any other Arab land.

The state was terribly poor. In 1926 the whole national budget totaled only eleven million dollars, but western companies had long been pumping oil in Iraq and Iran. Anglo-Persian Oil struck it rich in Kuwait. In 1931 Ibn Saud granted Standard of California permission to seek petroleum within his borders.

Saudi oil belonged exclusively to the king. So did everything else in the country. He called in a Belgian fiscal expert to help him organize his affairs, and one of the man's first proposals provided that the royal purse be kept apart from the national budget. This so enraged Ibn Saud that he ordered the Belgian beheaded. Mahmoud Bassiouni, president of Egypt's senate, traveled to Mecca and Riyadh to intercede on behalf of the Belgian expert, who was sent back home.

This incident has some historical value as an illustration of Ibn Saud's absolute power. He could and did do with his vast new wealth as he wished. Some went to maintaining a government and modernizing his army, but what reached the people arrived only as a byproduct of his main expenditures. The King had many wives—only four at any one time in strict accord with Islamic law—but many, and uncounted concubines.

Under Abdul Aziz and later his son, Saud ibn Saud, the royal treasury provided richly for wives, concubines, sons, grandchildren, servants, and slaves, and paid for palaces to house them all. King Saud, when he took the throne, displayed such fantastic extravagance and such brazen disregard of his people's needs that his name became a foul word in his subject's mouths. In 1965 his younger brother Faisal, supported by the clergy, forced Saud to get out and let Faisal rule as regent. Saud abdicated a little later and Faisal became king in name as well as in fact.

Faisal saw the need to modernize his kingdom but showed no more eagerness than his predecessors to abandon any of his power. His religious views were as rigid as those of any Wahabi mullah. Not even foreign diplomats at his court could serve or possess alcohol. Foreign women seen in public in clothing that the clergy considered immodest risked having their husbands expelled from the country. No Christian minister or priest could enter Saudi Arabia, even as a chaplain for a foreign embassy. No Jew was admitted in any capacity.

Once Abdul Aziz ibn Saud had feared to let the British get a toehold inside his kingdom, but his eagerness for oil money and (after 1945) his fear of revolution overcame that. He let the United States establish an air base at Dhahran—but required the Americans to screen every member of their forces to keep all Jews out of them. American Jews protested bitterly, but Washington took little heed. Greed for petroleum exercised far more influence than moral or legal scruples.

Faisal did inch his country forward. He slashed the huge allowances paid to the royal family and lived with one wife in a relatively modest palace. He freed his own slaves and urged others to do the same, but dared not order them to do so. He spent a tenth of his income on education and for a time new schools were reportedly being built at the rate of seventy a year. He even provided schools for girls, and paid the expenses of college study abroad for the sons of politically reliable families.

The Wahabi clergy fought his modernization program at every

step but could not quite stop it. New free clinics and hospitals cared for the sick, even among the Muslim pilgrims who came to Saudi Arabia to visit the holy cities of Medina and Mecca. Desalination plants and a program of water conservation improved the state's agriculture.

Faisal and the Revolution   Viewed alone these measures suggested important progress. As evidence of social progress or even social conscience, they were something altogether else. Faisal, like his father, was still a tribal patriarch without the compassion that marked the sheik of Kuwait. New paved highways and sprawling airports impressed those visitors who came from the west, but for workers in the cities and nomads in the desert stretches they offered almost nothing except a glimpse of a world they could not know. In lands ruled by despots that little bit of knowledge can often be dangerous.

Those Saudi Arabs who studied in foreign schools discovered new social, political, and economic horizons. Faisal's new schools needed teachers, and the only source of a plentiful supply of Arabic-speaking teachers was Egypt. While these young men bred in the Arab revolution taught Saudi youths to read and write, they implanted some of their own opinions and judgments. In the oil fields, too, workers absorbed new thoughts. King Faisal followed an Arab foreign policy both because he was himself Arab and because the fast-spreading sense of Arab kinship left him no alternative. He was especially bitter toward Israel and adamant on the subject of the Palestinians' rights, but inside the Arab world his opposition to the revolution and his fear of it dictated most of his decisions and actions.

In Yemen at one corner of his kingdom and Iraq at another the revolution was at his gates. He tried to stop the Yemeni revolution in its tracks with money, arms, and men, as his brother Saud had tried. He recruited and paid mercenaries to do some of the Yemeni royalists' fighting for them. When Egypt was in desperate financial straits after June 1967, he used the power of his wealth to deprive the Yemeni republic of Egyptian help by forcing Nasser to get out of Yemen and stay out. Yet the fact of successful revolution in Yemen mocked all his efforts.

Saudi monarchs were always leery of Egypt—they feared and envied her. Nasser in particular was the target of Saud and Faisal's enmity, and the former had often hatched and financed plots for his overthrow. But as matters go between Arabs, when Faisal assailed his half-brother Saud, the latter sought refuge in Cairo and Nasser gave him asylum.

Faisal's determination to protect his throne and his power, and the American grip on Saudi oil, tied him naturally to the United States even while the United States continued to guard and finance his Zionist enemies. His tacit alliance with Israel's sponsor alienated many of his own people, especially within the army. Saudi military men were ardent nationalists like others in their profession and many of them were broadening their nationalism to include all the hundred millions in the Arab world.

Events revealed the paradoxical character of Faisal's policies. He sought on the one hand to give his state all the benefits of the technological wizardry of the west. On the other hand he guarded the ultraconservative Wahabism and sought to preserve the political attitudes of a long dead past. The *Manchester Guardian* commented that his "attempt to secure the economic benefits of a modernized industrial society while preserving the rigid moral code of [Wahabi] Islam is about as likely to be successful as an Arabian King Canute trying to hold back the drifting sands of the desert."

23: AROUND THE RIM OF ARABIA
Of oil
and politics

THE 1956 Suez episode forecast the end of the British empire in the Arab world. The proud little island on whose dominion the sun never set was now just another European state, but neither her leaders nor her people were yet prepared to accept that fact. Ghandi's campaign of passive disobedience had forced Britain out of the Indian subcontinent. The Zionists had pushed her out of Palestine. Egypt was free, and Iraq was gone. Jordan's king had fired a British general and all his countrymen. South Africa was an independent republic, and Rhodesia refused to acknowledge British rule. Little groups of islands scattered through the oceans proclaimed their independence.

ADEN

Only the Aden region and a chain of sheikdoms in the Persian Gulf remained to Britain from her centuries of imperial glory.

The United States hoped that Britain could hang on at Aden. The United States had eclipsed British influence elsewhere in the Arab lands, but Washington was happy to have British ships and soldiers patrol the Red Sea and the Persian Gulf. It saved the United States from having to take on that task. Those waters were extremely important and the reason was oil. Some of the gulf sheikdoms were very rich in oil, and Aden had earth's largest petroleum refinery and research complex.

Britain had been there since 1837, when she occupied the island of Perim. In 1839 she took Aden. She managed each little enclave separately as she pushed up the shore of the gulf because fragmentation made control easier. In the middle decades of the twentieth century, however, the cost of individual administration grew prohibitive and in 1936 she attempted to bring her South Arabian holdings into a federal union ruled from Aden. Tribal feuds and fierce opposition inside Aden defeated the scheme, but in 1958 she tried it again.

The (Charles) Johnston Plan   Yemeni farmers and herdsmen loyal to tribal sheiks peopled the outlying areas. Aden itself was home to seamen, dockworkers, refinery employees, street cleaners, artisans, and petty merchants. It was also the seat of British government and the residence of military men and rich foreign traders. The foreign presence was a festering abscess.

British policed Aden's streets. Europeans dominated the city's business, managed its industry, and held every important job. Adeni Arabs eked out their meager existence in the ghettos of Crater Town and Sheikh Othman. Every circumstance of Adeni life bred hatred of the white master race. Because local patriotism would have been a futile thing, Adeni Arabs were among the first to espouse the Arab nationalism preached by Gamal Abdul Nasser. British border wars with Yemen reinforced hatred of the west.

Continuing disorder created a critical situation. The British sought to erect a string of petty rural sheikdoms around the city, hoping they could hold Adeni Arabs in check for them.

Britain's plan for the Aden region became the Johnston Plan, named for the governor, Sir Charles Johnston. A new South Arabian Federation would govern Aden and surrounding shiekdoms. A municipal administration staffed by selected and docile natives would run the city, and the tribal chiefs in the back country would have considerable local autonomy. The sheiks would form a federal council with Johnston sitting at the top.

The municipal council approved this plan September 25, 1962, seven to five. On September 26 in Sana'a the republic of Yemen was proclaimed by Abdullah al Sallal. Historically and geographically Aden was part of Yemen. Johnston wrote of the council vote:

If the Yemeni revolution had come one day earlier or the Legislative Council vote one day later, I feel pretty certain that [the federation plan] would never have received the votes of a majority.[1]

"On so chancy a basis," the *Manchester Guardian* commented, does British policy in South Arabia rest."[2]

The life of the federation was short. The sheiks distrusted Great Britain and each other. Adeni Arabs resented them all. London realized that some day the Union Jack would come down at Aden, as already it had fallen in so many other places, and she promised ultimate independence. The Arabs in Aden demanded to know—independence when and for whom?

Abject poverty combined with hatred of Britain turned Adenis into revolutionaries as well as Arab nationalists. To them Arab nationalism and the Arab revolution were one. Death and hunger haunted them. In December 1963 an Adeni gunman tried to kill the governor, and British police filled their jails with suspected foes of the federation. Arabs said the British were using torture to squeeze out the names of nationalists still at large; Amnesty International, a world body devoted to guarding the interests of political prisoners, said the accusations were true. The United Nations General Assembly (in which the west no longer enjoyed an automatic majority) demanded release of the

habitants or killing them, as at Deir Yasin. The Zionists founded a state and called it Israel. They occupied areas far outside the boundaries established by the United Nations, and western governments (in the beginning even the Soviet Union) accepted their conquests, then took them into the United Nations.

Every Arab state refused to concede that Israel had a legal right to survive as a political entity or that the United Nations had the moral or legal authority to dispose of other peoples' homeland without regard for the right of self-determination. They refused even to talk of peace with the new Israel. A treaty of peace is an agreement between sovereign nations in which both begin by recognizing the other's lawful existence and its legal and moral authority to discuss, as between equals, all the questions at issue. To enter into any kind of deal with Israel, therefore, would have been to abandon the basic Arab position on Palestine. There could be no peace at that price.

Through two decades after the founding of Israel warfare went on intermittently. In virtually every instance the Israelis won temporary victories because their armies were better trained, better led, and better armed. But their military supremacy could not be traded for legitimacy.

The Arab states had many times the population of Israel, but numbers alone were not enough. As previously noted, Britain and France had purposely kept native Arab armies weak; they dared not permit the development of forces that might challenge their imperial power. The only exception had been in Jordan where the British, sure of their grip, established and themselves led the best army in the Arab world, the Arab Legion —yet even the Legion was kept too small to pose much danger.

France was gone from Lebanon and Syria. Lebanon, however, was too small, too weak, and too deeply concerned with her profitable western trade to matter much militarily. In Syria the bitter struggle between nationalist ambitions and the banker-merchant-priest coalition guaranteed a constant state of turmoil. Not until 1954 did Britain leave Egypt, and there the problems of a new revolutionary program left the country without money or adequate military leadership.

Yet despite their handicaps these weak Arab countries refused to make any slightest concessions.

It is a rule of thumb in world affairs that when intolerable political and economic problems defy solution by any other means, one side or the other resorts to war. War is the last resort of politico-economic conflict. Within this framework the government of Israel had to go yet another round of warfare.

Forward to War   Jordan and Syria were the easiest targets. Egypt lay beyond the vast Sinai desert, and a screen of United Nations soldiers held the Sinai and Gaza borders. Moreover, the UNEF presence appeared to assure the Israelis protection against any attack from Egypt in support of the other two states. Syria had a military alliance with Egypt, but at the moment that fact seemed unimportant.

Jordan held the fertile west bank of the Jordan River, and Israel wanted that region not only as farmland for new Jewish immigrants but because the river offered a more easily defensible frontier. She coveted the Golan Heights because those hills frowned down on her own territory and offered Syrian and Palestinian forces a considerable military advantage.

During the first weeks of 1967 five serious clashes erupted along Israel's Syrian border, and several tank battles took place. Under United Nations pressure the two sides met January 29 and accepted a new truce, but United Nations participants in the talks made no bones about their judgment that the Israelis had been chiefly responsible for the fighting. After new clashes Israel refused to take part in further discussions.[1] Syrian and Israeli aircraft met in a series of battles east of Lake Tiberias on April 8.[2] On May 9 the Israeli Knesset authorized direct military action against Syria.[3]

Soviet and Syrian intelligence reported that Israel was massing ten to fourteen brigades in the north. Apparently this report was not wholly accurate, but at the time the claim could not be ignored. Syria demanded that Egypt honor her commitment to go to war under the terms of their alliance.

Egypt's Nasser faced a serious problem. He could not reject Syria's demand without a loss of personal prestige and his position as recognized leader of the Arab world, yet neither could he go to Syria's aid while United Nations forces patrolled his boundaries with Israel.

UNEF occupied positions inside Egypt under an agreement made in 1956 by Nasser and United Nations Secretary-General Dag Hammarskjöld. Israel had refused to permit United Nations troops on her side of the border and had no part whatever, legal or moral, in the Nasser-Hammarskjöld deal.

It is particularly important to remember that UNEF was permitted into Egypt only on Nasser's tolerance. Neither its commander nor the United Nations itself had any rights there beyond such as Egypt granted. As guests they were bound to leave when Egypt withdrew her permission for them to stay, and the secretary-general pulled out the UNEF contingents at Nasser's request because he had no choice.[4] Sixty thousand Egyptian troops moved up to the Sinai and Gaza borders, but Nasser was seriously handicapped by the fact that forty thousand or more of his best men, with their planes and equipment, were in Yemen. They had been dispatched to protect the new revolutionary government there. On May 22 President Nasser proclaimed a blockade of the Strait of Tiran and forbade all Israeli shipping and any vessels carrying strategic cargo to or from Israel to use the waterway.[5]

On May 23 United States President Lyndon Johnson declared that every state in the Arab region must respect the territorial integrity of every other.[6] Later, on June 19, after Israel had seized great chunks of Arab land, he spoke out for the right of each of these states to live in peace but dropped his demand for their territorial rights.

Tiran and the Law   In United Nations debate the United States and Israel argued that Secretary-General U Thant should

sending Vice-President Mohieddin to meet with President
Lyndon B. Johnson for talks scheduled on June 7. Johnson had
secured a commitment from Israel not to attack or disturb their
talks for at least two weeks. In his memoirs published in 1971
(*The Vantage Point*, pp. 289–303) Johnson admits to the double-
cross but never explains why he had kept it a well-hidden secret,
like the secret reports on how Israel deliberately bombed and
strafed the USS Liberty—to conceal who started the 1967 war.
Once again the world was deceived.

June 5   In the small hours of Monday, June 5, 1967, an
Israeli air armada struck Egypt's home airfields and destroyed
or damaged almost every military plane there before any of them
could get off the ground. Paratroops landed at Sharm al Sheik.
Ground forces seized the Gaza Strip. Israeli brigades stationed
in the north swept to the bank of the Jordan River and moved
against the Golan Heights. Jordanian troops in Jerusalem put
up a good fight but lost the Arab sector of that city.

At New York the Security Council voted unanimously to
demand a cease fire. The four warring states agreed and fighting
stopped everywhere except in Syria. There the Israelis had not
yet won all their objectives and continued until these had been
achieved. Israel then held all the Golan Heights area and a
battle front only forty miles from Damascus.

Egyptian troops retreating through Sinai took terrible pun-
ishment from the air. At Cairo President Nasser, speaking on
television, assumed personal responsibility for this new disaster and offered to resign. A fantastic outpouring of public
support urged him to stay in office and the national assembly
rejected his resignation.[11]

Jubilant Israelis and their western followers tagged this brief
struggle the Six Day War. The term is still used. That was an
almost grotesque misnomer. It was in fact no more than the
latest outbreak of open warfare in a conflict that had already
lasted nineteen years and bade fair to continue for many more.

Israel occupied all of the Sinai peninsula, the Gaza region, the whole of Palestine west of the Jordan River, and a portion of Syria, an area four times as large as the Zionist state had held on June 4. Within the newly conquered territory was a vast number of hostile Arabs with new reasons for bitterness. How many of these Arabs there might be, nobody knew. The Israeli government said that they numbered about a million. Less biased observers placed the figure fifty percent higher.

Search for Peace   The Security Council had a new topic of discussion now: not how to stop a war but how to end it. The talk seemed endless and futile. Still arrayed on opposite sides were the Soviet Union and the United States.

Israel renewed her demands for direct negotiations with her Arab foes, and in America, particularly, public opinion supported this position, as if there were somehow special magic in the mere act of talking. Few, even among those who should have known better, seemed to understand that face-to-face talks—carrying with them a tacit recognition of Israel's legal right to discuss the problems of the Arab region on a basis of sovereign equality—had in fact been a principal Israeli goal since 1949. The mere achievement of an agreement for direct talks would have been a tremendous victory for the Zionist state, and this was a triumph that no Arab leader dared to yield. At stake, from the Arab viewpoint, was the prime claim that Israel had no moral or legal right to any voice in regional affairs.

At the United Nations sentiment was almost unanimous that a start toward peace must begin with total Israeli withdrawal from the lands occupied in June, but this was a step that Israel refused even to consider. The government at Tel Aviv declared emphatically that Israel would never return to the pre-1967 boundaries.[12] Egypt, Jordan, and Syria refused to consider any discussion of peace until all captured territory had been evacuated.

Israel and her western Zionist supporters—even the government of the United States—preferred to ignore the long established rule of international law that military conquest does not confer political sovereignty. Every recognized authority agrees on this point,[13] and every empire-bent power in the world has honored that principle at least in form. When France and Great Britain established colonies and protectorates in the lands of Asia and Africa, they made sure to get the signatures of local rulers on some kind of treaty that acknowledged the Europeans' right to move in. Sometimes it was necessary to depose or eliminate one ruler and set a more pliant one in his place, but in the end there was always a signature on some kind of document to justify the imperialist presence. An expanding United States had signed dozens of such treaties with Indian tribes from Massachusetts to Washington; every one was ultimately broken by the conquering Americans, but the initial legalities had at least been observed. Israel had no semblance of consent from those she conquered, and it was very clear that she never would have through a foreseeable future.

The Security Council recognized its inability to act and turned the thorny issue over to the General Assembly where no government had a veto. The United States, aware of its weakness in that body, refused to join in a call for a special session of the Assembly, but a substantial majority of Assembly members (including twenty-seven Afro-Asian states) convened the meeting. The determination of the United States to continue to support the Israeli view was illustrated by the fact that the American delegate to the United Nations was a lifelong Zionist, Arthur Goldberg.

At Jerusalem Israel began to remove every vestige of Arab character in that part of the city previously held by Jordan and make it a wholly Jewish community. Tens of thousands of Arabs were evicted from their homes, and public housing projects erected by the thousands. Israel made Jerusalem—a city sacred to Jew, Christian, and Muslim alike—its seat of government. The general assembly by a vote of 116 (Israel and the United States abstained) declared in 1967 that Israel's annexation of Jerusalem was inadmissable. Israel went right ahead with bulldozers and new settlements. By 1971 over one hundred thousand had already moved in and a ten thousand-unit apartment complex was in the completion stages.

President De Gaulle of France denounced both Israel and the United States for their roles in the 1967 events and broke diplomatic relations with the Israelis. This change of attitude marked the first open defection from what had previously been a solid western phalanx of support for the Zionist cause. The Israeli parliament authorized the government to annex the Jordanian sector of Jerusalem.[14]

From a bitter round of debate in the General Assembly two proposed resolutions emerged. One, offered by Latin American countries acting for the United States, called for Israeli evacuation of the newly conquered territories, the internationalization of Jerusalem, and an end to the state of belligerency between the warring countries, to be followed by direct negotiations and a settlement of all outstanding differences.

The second, proposed by Yugoslavia with support from India and other Afro-Asian countries, made no mention of the state of belligerency or talks. It demanded Israeli evacuation of the seized lands and urged every United Nations member-state to help the Secretary-General implement this program.

The Yugoslav proposal frightened both Israel and the United States. Its call for the help of United Nations states in forcing Israeli withdrawal had been lifted almost verbatim from the Security Council measure jammed through in 1950 by the United States to allow United Nations forces into Korea. Under its terms the Soviet Union would have had United Nations sanction for direct military intervention in the Arab-Israeli conflict.[15]

The two measures came to a vote July 4, 1967. The Yugoslav measure drew 53 ayes, 46 nays, and 20 abstentions. The Latin American proposal attracted 56 favorable votes, 43 in opposition, and the same 20 abstentions. Because as a "substantive question" either would have required a two-thirds majority of those voting, both failed.[16]

The Security Council took up the problem once more. It was clear now that the United States could no longer enforce its will in the Council, and America began to hedge on her all-out support of Israel. On November 22, 1967, the Council by unanimous vote adopted resolution no. 242, which stated in part:

> *Emphasizing: the inadmissability of the acquisition of territory by war. . . . Affirms: (i) Withdrawal of Israeli forces from territory occupied in the recent conflict.*[17]

The measure recognized Israel's right to exist as a sovereign state within her old borders and called upon Egypt to permit the unhindered passage of all nations' ships through international waterways under her control. Since that day all attempts by states outside the Arab region to establish peace there have been predicated on this measure, leaving the Israelis with no international support whatever for their determination to hang onto lands they have seized.

Once more, nothing happened. Israel refused to budge. Egypt could not in any event act upon the United Nations call for action on Tiran and Suez. The Israelis held Sharm al Sheik and the east bank of the canal. Once, when Egyptian engineers tried to survey the canal with a view to clearing away the block ships sunk there in 1967, Israeli artillery drove their boat back to their own side of the waterway.

Jerusalem   The old Testament speaks of Jerusalem as the city of the Canaanite, an Arab tribe, when David conquered it in the tenth century B.C. (II Samuel 5:5–3). It was Salem, an Arabic name, as early as when Abraham went into Palestine some four thousand years ago (Genesis 14:18) and was then ruled by King Melchizedek, a Canaanite. A tablet discovered at Tel-El-Amarna, etched in the fourteenth century B.C., spoke of Salem's King Abd Kimiba, an Egyptian. Some fifteen hundred years ago the mother of Emperor Constantine started the custom of pilgrimage to Jerusalem as the birthplace of Christianity.

The second khalif, Omar ibn El-Khattab, defeated the Romans who occupied Palestine in A.D. 638. When he entered Jerusalem he descended from his horse and walked on foot in reverence, but before walking inside he made history's first treaty to protect freedom of religion. Under Patriarch Sophronius were placed all shrines, churches, and religious matters of the Christians. He guaranteed the human and religious rights of all Christians, residents and pilgrims, and pledged security of their homes and holy places. They were exempted from taxation by Muslim rulers and the pledge was binding for all time. He also rescinded the Roman decree of A.D. 135 which banished Jews from Jerusalem and allowed them to return and exercise their faith as a people of the book. Few did.

Omar ibn El-Khattab recalled that at one time in the days of Prophet Muhammad all Muslims faced Jerusalem in their five daily prayers, and it was from Jerusalem that the Prophet ascended to Heaven. A mosque, Masjid al-Aqsa, treasured by Muslims all over the world was built in 688 to commemorate that event. Omar built a mosq known as the dome of the Rock, and it too stands as a Muslim symbol. Christian shrines are many and too well known to recount, but one historic fact is that the keys to the Church of the Holy Sepulchre have for generations been in the custody of a Muslim Arab family.

The 1947 United Nations partition internationalized Jerusalem, but the war of 1947–48 brought Jordanian troops to defend the city. They stayed, denying Jews free access to their shrines, specifically the Wailing Wall. On June 7, 1967, Israel occupied and annexed Jerusalem. On July 5, the U.N. General Assembly by a vote of 99–0 (20 abstentions) declared the action invalid under international law. On July 14 another resolution was passed, viewing with deep concern Israel's ignoring of the prohibition to annex occupied territory. On May 21, 1968, the Security Council passed a similar resolution. On all three votes the United States abstained, and Israel ignored the resolutions. She announced a policy of "total Judaization" of Jerusalem— massive seizure of Arab lands, demolition and bull-dozing of Arab houses and properties, thus flagrantly violating the Geneva Convention of 1949 which prohibited the transfer of population and settlement of occupied territory. On August 10, 1971, Israeli Defense Minister Moshe Dayan spoke there of restoring Jerusalem to the perfect picture of "Eretz Israel," the Zionist dream of a Jewish kingdom although it had existed for only seventy out of the several thousand years of Palestine and Jerusalem history.

The political reality lies in what Israel calls "making facts." After the removal of Arab Christians and Muslims from Jerusalem came the massive building, settlement of Jews in Arab quarters, and surrounding of the city. These housing projects offended the aesthetic sense even of Jewish city planners and architects, and the Israeli Daily Ha'aretz warned that it would transform the city "into a kind of Los Angeles." Ignoring United Nations resolutions, international law, and morality Israel moved the capitol to Jerusalem to prove that she intended to stay. This, leaders said, was non-negotiable.

The United Nations Security Council on September 25, 1971, passed unopposed U.N. Document S/RES/298 (1971). The resolution stated *inter alia:*

1. *Reaffirms* Security Council resolutions 252 (1968) and 267 (1969);

2. *Deplores* the failure of Israel to respect the previous resolutions adopted by the United Nations concerning measures and actions by Israel purporting to affect the status of the city of Jerusalem;

3. *Confirms* in the clearest possible terms that all legislative and administrative actions taken by Israel to change the

status of the city of Jerusalem, including expropriation of land and properties, transfer of populations, and legislation aimed at the incorporation of the occupied section are totally invalid and cannot change that status;

4. *Urgently calls upon* Israel to rescind all previous measures and actions and to take no further steps in the occupied section of Jerusalem which may purport to change the status of the City, or which would prejudice the rights of the inhabitants, and the interests of the international community or a just and lasting peace;

5. *Requests* the Secretary-General in consultation with the President of the Security Council and using such instrumentalities as he may choose, including a representative or a mission, to report to the Security Council as appropriate, and in any event within 60 days, on the implementation of this resolution.

Two days later the Jewish Telegraphic Agency reported that the Israeli government "will not enter into discussions with any political factor on the basis of the resolution."

Problems of Conquest   The people and government of Israel began to realize that their great military triumph had in fact created more problems than it had solved, and one of the most troublesome was the presence of a vast number of hostile Arabs.

As in 1948–49 there were three possible ways to cope with the situation. In 1967 with the horrors of the Nazi campaign against Jews a generation gone, world opinion would no longer tolerate wholesale extermination of unassimilable Arabs. Israel tried expelling them, but an international outcry demanded the readmission of those who wished to return and Israel went through the motions of seeming willing to receive them back. Only a very few, however, were permitted to cross back into Israeli-held territory.

The only feasible control left to the Israelis had to be conciliation or subjugation. Conciliation was impossible; Palestinian Arabs in the mass refused to be mollified, and Israeli opinion was in no mood for peaceful coexistence. The consequence was a fierce, continuing effort by the government and its army to compel Palestinian acceptance of the Arabs' status as scarcely tolerated residents.

Israeli Expansionism   At the 1919 peace conference which adopted the Balfour Declaration as western policy, Zionist spokesmen proposed for their planned Jewish state boundaries that took in much of Sinai (including the shore of the Gulf of Aqaba and the Strait of Tiran), both sides of the Jordan River, almost half of Lebanon, and more of Syria than Israel won in 1967. After Israel was established, chauvinist expansionists talked of a state that would embrace all the land from the Euphrates to the Nile—territory that the ancient state of Israel had in fact once ruled briefly. Some politicians encouraged these ambitions. On June 8, 1967, while the invasion of Arab neighbor states was in progress, Prime Minister Levi Eshkol declared that the new military situation established "a new political reality" and that the newly seized areas were already part of the Zionist state.

Mere conquest, however, is neither consolidation nor assimilation. The newly seized lands had to be policed; and newly established boundaries had to be guarded. Protecting these regions against Arab retaliation and internal dissension demanded money and men. Soldiers had to be fed and clothed, sheltered and paid, as well as armed. Many who had been called away from their civilian tasks for war duty had to be kept in service for the job of occupation.

Modern war requires technical skills equal to those of peaceful industry and the long standing Ashkenazi practice of keeping the Sephardim in subservient roles began to backfire. Afro-Asian Jews had been denied an opportunity to gain the knowledge and skills available to Ashkenazim, and now thousands of jobs vacated by military reservists could not be filled. This imposed new burdens on an already weak and staggering economy.

Israel was the most heavily taxed country on earth, yet taxes continued to rise. Every worker, after his large income tax was deducted, had to pay out a tithe of his wages for a national defense loan. Import duties went up and up and government laid new restrictions on the goods admitted. Export sales, despite desperate efforts, could not keep pace with the military budget, already eating twenty percent of the gross national product.

The most dangerous weakness in Israel's economy was the import surplus—excess of imports over exports. In 1970 Israel bought foreign goods and services that cost $1.265 billion more than she earned with exports. In 1967 her holdings of foreign currency were $976 million; in 1970 they were only $467 million, including the vast sums received as loans, gifts, and bond sales from abroad (chiefly in the United States). This deficit persisted despite the half billion dollar credit voted by the United States Congress in 1970 and another $52.1 million from America for the purchase of agricultural products.[18]

Immigration   European Jews still controlled the political and economic apparatus but their ratio in the total Jewish population was falling disastrously. Western Jews refused to migrate to Israel in numbers large enough to restore Ashkenazi superiority, and there remained only one possible source of Ashkenazi immigrants: some three million Jews in the Soviet Union.

Israeli spokesmen and western Zionists began a vigorous campaign to persuade or compel the USSR to let those Jews go to Israel. The United States, historically imbued with virulent anticommunism, became the principal arena for this program. Zionist pickets appeared at every hall and theater in which Soviet representatives or performers were scheduled. The extremist Jewish Defense League bombed and burned Soviet offices and motor cars and harassed Soviet officials in New York and Washington. Editors and commentators committed to the Zionist cause thundered against the USSR's reluctance to open its gates for Jews who might wish to migrate to Israel. In March 1971 Zionist leaders from several countries held a thoroughly publicized conference aimed at helping to get Ashkenazi Jews out of Russia.

Few outside the Israeli government appear to have realized the purpose of this program. Certainly the United States public got no hint of it. The Zionist rulers of Israel desperately needed new Ashkenazi settlers to keep their political and economic power, and inside Russia were enough Ashkenazim to protect the grip of Israel's European bosses. There was no question of Russian Jews going to the United States, France, or any country other than Israel.

Soviet rulers had sound reason to resist this campaign. Their government was firmly committed to the Arab cause against Israel and it was not their purpose to strengthen the Arabs' enemy. They were also aware that the swift decline and probable disappearance of Ashkenazi Zionist control inside Israel could well do more to end the bitter Arab-Israeli conflict and produce a viable peace than any other plan yet proposed.

Meanwhile, however, the USSR had other fish to fry. Moscow needed a period of reasonably amicable coexistence with the west to improve the lot of her own people, build better relations with countries such as West Germany, and look at her Chinese borders where some one million troops were poised for eventualities.

Some Soviet Jews were therefore permitted to emigrate. Conflicting propaganda made it impossible to determine how many Russian Jews might wish to leave, but the Israeli hope of winning large numbers was fatuous. At the same time the number of potential emigrants to Israel was probably greater than the USSR was ready to admit. Available and credible estimates suggested that during 1971 several thousand Jews would go from the Soviet Union to Israel, but that number—or even several times as many—would neither affect the Arab-Israeli military balance nor bolster the Ashkenazi position inside Israel enough to matter much.

Several groups of Zionist Jews within the USSR were hauled into court for anti-Soviet activities and for trying to hijack aircraft to get them to Israel, and these trials earned reams of anti-Russian publicity in the United States. The cynical observer could note that when Arabs hijacked western planes, the incidents were protrayed as vicious crimes against all humanity. When Zionist Jews adopted similar tactics, their activities became almost heroic struggles against Russian oppression. It was a matter of whose ox was being gored.

Israel was no longer a land of immigrants. Informed estimates in the absence of accurate figures indicate that in 1971 more than half of the Jewish population—both Ashkenazi and Sephardi—was native born and that of these native Israelis a majority was of Afro-Asian origin. The Ashkenazim, with their European background, had a much lower birth rate than the Sephardim.

Because Israel was their birthplace, these people were disposed to be nationalists. They called themselves Sabras. Their roots in this corner of the Arab world made them less antagonistic toward their Arab neighbors even though the state into which they were born had been fighting Arabs for more than two decades. They were frankly less religious than the founders of Israel and had no interest in maintaining a Jewish theocratic state. It was their hope in time to find some means of living at peace with their Arab neighbors, and even to be part of that region.

For the moment, however, the Sabras could not exercise the potential influence of their numbers. Few of them had entered the political arena to shape Israel's future.

26: THE PALESTINIANS GO TO WAR

Refugees turn fedayeen

SINCE the birth of Israel in 1948 some of the bolder Palestinians in Jordan, Gaza, Lebanon, and Syria had been conducting guerilla operations against the Israelis on a minor scale. In the beginning their attacks had been little more than pinpricks because they were neither numerous nor well planned. The men who carried out these raids were organized in a variety of local groups, most of them with no military training at all and only such arms as they could steal, scrounge, or make.

Within the camps on Israel's rim most Palestinians still counted themselves refugees. They joined one or another of the political parties that vied for support among them and did little else than shout boastful slogans; they listened to Radio Cairo and other Arab voices and waited for the established Arab states to keep their pledge that the Zionists would be pushed into the sea and Palestine restored to its rightful owners. Meanwhile they subsisted on the pennies per day doled out by the United Nations Relief Works Agency and put their hope in the homeless children they sired. When Egypt, the Soviet Union, and

268

the United Nations General Assembly forced Israel, Britain, and France to pull out of Sinai and Suez in 1956–57, they cheered mightily, but these events improved their lot not at all.

After the 1967 debacle refugees in their squalid camps began to realize that their faith in Nasser and the other Arab rulers was misplaced. The able and thoughtful among them reached the reluctant conclusion that, if Palestine were to become an Arab land again, the Palestinians would have to do the job themselves. New and stronger guerilla organizations began to take shape, and young men flocked to join them. The quality of their training improved, and the number and severity of their raids and attacks increased.

In 1964 the Arab League had approved the creation of a Palestine Liberation Organization with headquarters at Cairo. Ahmad Shukairy, a Palestinian who had served in the United Nations as a representative for both Syria and Saudi Arabia, was named to head it. PLO attracted thousands of recruits, chiefly from the Gaza region, and its members got some military training, principally in Egypt. The organization won a considerable following among Palestinians in Jordan, too, and in the Israeli sweep of June 1967 its units fought well, but the magnitude of the Israeli victory virtually wiped PLO out of existence. Shukairy himself remained at Amman while the fighting continued and, when new commando groups emerged after June, his prestige reached the vanishing point. The era of a Palestinian movement under the control or influence of any Arab state or leader had gone—as had the exclusivity of the notion of liberation. Now an all-encompassing revolutionary blue print was part of the aim of the struggle.

The Resistance Movement   No accurate record has become available of the number of Palestinian guerillas in organizations that began to be effectively active after the June hostilities. At least seventeen separate groups have been identified by observers, but only four achieved real importance.

Largest of these was Al Fatah*, the Palestinian Liberation Movement. It began to take shape at Damascus between 1964 and 1967, conducted propaganda in the refugee camps, and published a small magazine, *Palestine*. After the 1967 disaster Al Fatah transferred to Amman. The king and his government knew the Palestinians were directing and executing their operations from inside Jordan but did not then dare to interfere; a majority of Hussein's nominal subjects were Palestinians, and any premature move against them, after his disastrous defeat at the hands of Israel, seemed likely to bring his own downfall.

The recognized leader of Al Fatah was a Palestinian educated in Egypt. For a few months he concealed his identity under the *nom de guerre* of Abu Ammar before he came into the open as Yasir Arafat.

In the beginning his program demanded only the restoration of Arab rule in Palestine. He was himself a conservative in political and economic affairs but kept his movement free of ideological bias, much as the Committee of Free Officers had first done in Egypt and the National Liberation Front had done in Algeria. This attracted men of all political hues, and Al Fatah quickly became the largest and strongest of the Palestinian resistance movements.

By 1970, however, both Arafat and Al Fatah changed their attitude. The examples of the revolutionary Arab states, faced with the need to reorder not only a political system but the national economy as well, made it obvious that the new state of Palestine at which Al Fatah aimed, would be compelled to adopt revolutionary methods of reorganization, and before 1970 dawned Arafat and Al Fatah were calling their movement the Palestinian revolution. In Algeria and Egypt many Arab leaders had accepted a similar change in attitude because circumstance left them no alternative. With recognition and financial support

* The word is a transliteration of the initials in Arabic of the Movement for the Liberation of Palestine.

from established Arab governments Fatah became the least revolutionary of the lot.

PFLP   The second largest resistance force until 1970 called itself the Popular Front for the Liberation of Palestine. PFLP began in Syria, too, with a coalition of several smaller groups. Its leader, George Habash, was an out-and-out Marxist, with close ties to the Nureddin al Atassi regime at Damascus. The strongest bases were in the refugee camps in Lebanon and Syria, and the following in Jordan or Gaza was only modest.

PFLP, attached to Marxist doctrine, aimed its principal blows at the Israeli economy. Its plans were on the grandiose side. Interfering with air traffic to and from Israel by hijacking aircraft, PFLP leaders believed they would frighten foreign planes out of the Israeli trade and discourage people of all nationalities from traveling to and from Israel by air.

Operatives did hijack and even destroy some aircraft. A PFLP attack on an Israeli plane on the ground at Athens provided the Israelis with an excuse for their helicopter raid on the Beirut airport December 28, 1968. In Switzerland, Greece, and Italy local authorities jailed PFLP agents for their activities, but in Arab countries (and especially in the refugee camps) popular sentiment acclaimed their campaign. New followers were won more rapidly than by any other liberation group until the civil war in Jordan in 1970, which is discussed at length in the next chapter. By then the Democratic Front emerged as the most revolutionary group and attracted some disenchanted Fatah and PFLP adherents.

Al Saïqa   One other Palestinian resistance organization grew large and important enough to deserve special notice. Al Saïqa (the Thunderbolt), like Al Fatah and the Popular Front, was born in Syria, where the governmental climate favored Palestinian rebels. Like PFLP, Saïqa drew most of its followers from the refugee centers in Syria and Lebanon. Former Syrian army officers led most of its small but tough military units, and its commandos received some military training with the Syrian forces. After 1970 Syria sharply cut its help to Al Saïqa, and Lebanon curtailed its operations. A splinter section broke off and operated independently of Damascus.

Guerilla War   As the French learned in Indochina and Algeria, as United States generals learned in Vietnam, even strong orthodox military forces can be outwitted and defeated by well-led guerillas in a country where the orthodox army is regarded by the local citizenry as a hostile power. Zionist guerillas—Haganah, Irgun Zvai Leumi, and the Stern Gang—had demonstrated this fact to the British in Palestine after World War II when they forced Great Britain to abandon her mandate there. The lessons of Mao's guerilla tactics were not lost.

The guerilla fights alone or in small groups. He cannot and does not stand against conventional armed forces in pitched battle. To be successful he must operate in a friendly region where the civilian population furnishes recruits, supplies food, stores weapons and ammunition, and provides shelter. He strikes his enemy secretly, then fades back into the native population.

In the refugee camps of Jordan, Lebanon, and Syria, and in the crowded Gaza Strip, guerilla forces had their sources of men and food and the security of anonimity but, until after the resistance organizations were ready to act together, they accomplished little. They raided Israeli settlements near the border, mined roads, ambushed patrols, bombed public buildings and marketplaces in Israeli towns—even busy Tel Aviv—but the political effect of their depredations was minor.

At the United Nations and in the chancelleries of the western governments they won no attention at all. To politicians, correspondents, editors, and the general public they remained only what they had been for two decades, refugees, with no identity of their own and no recognized national rights. When they fought for their rights, they were called "terrorists" and were dealt with as common criminals.

With Israel leading the way and the United States coming in strong on the refrain, the favored solution for the refugee problem was to redistribute the Palestinians through the various Arab countries, thus putting the constant reminders of their suffering and the wrongs against them comfortably out of sight.

There was no logic in this position, but logic is often abandoned for political expediency. The western world could believe that Jews all over earth preserved for more than eighteen hundred years the memory of what had once been a Hebrew land and yearned to go back there. Yet that same western world believed that Palestinian Arabs uprooted from their ancestral homeland, living within sight and sound of their homes and their fields, would accept in meek silence transfer to some other country, as the Acadians of Nova Scotia let themselves be transported to Louisiana. In these terms the stubborn resistance of the Palestinians is easier to understand.[1]

As early as 1963 United States officials persuaded President Habib Bourguiba of Tunisia to propose the resettlement of the Palestinians, and Israel's Abba Eban responded with an essay in *Foreign Affairs*[2] offering Israel's financial help for such an undertaking.

American officials and even the readers of United States newspapers knew that the Palestinians would accept nothing less than a return to their homes. Laurence Michelmore, UNRWA administrator of the Arab refugee problem, had told one American newsman in 1965 that the Palestinians hated Israel as the direct author of their misery, Britain for shepherding the Zionists into Palestine, and the United States for fostering and protecting the Jewish state.[3] Other correspondents who visited the camps sent back similar reports.[4] As early as 1966 reporters were warning that the bitterness of the refugees posed a serious potential threat to peace.[5] At the same time U.S. senators dependent on Zionist votes were complaining that the refugee relief rolls were loaded with false names and demanding cuts in American contributions to the UNRWA budget.[6]

The Israeli invasion of three Arab countries in 1967 stunned most Palestinians in the refugee camps. Their abiding faith in the promises of Gamal Abdul Nasser and other Arab rulers died. The 1967 warfare also gave the Israelis a new refugee problem. Many of the Palestinians in Jordan's West Bank region—some of them already refugees from the 1948 conflict—fled across the Jordan River to new sanctuaries in Arab-ruled territory, but others stayed where they were, and Israel faced the need to feed and shelter them with or without UNRWA help.

1967   At this point Palestinians of every political complexion —Christians and Muslims alike—were ready to abandon all hope of help from the established Arab states. Recovering their homeland was now their own task. As the principal liberation organizations increased their activities, they found a ready welcome from those who once had been only refugees but were suddenly become a militant, determined people. Reports sent home by foreign journalists of the political attitudes of the Palestinians inside her borders drove Israel to impose new restrictions on the press in an effort to keep the facts from reaching the outside world.[7]

Karameh   A small dusty village on the east bank of the Jordan River was a training base for Al Fatah. In March 1968 an Israeli armed column attacked it, and probably the largest battle of that war took place. Some one hundred fedayeen and thirty-two Israeli soldiers died. The word *karama* in Arabic means honor, and the closeness of the words helped make Karameh a symbol of Arab popular resistance.

Al Fatah   A British correspondent in Jordan set out to discover the truth about the strength and attitudes of the men who were flocking to join Al Fatah.[8] Officers at the group's Amman headquarters sent him to a camp near the Jordanian capital. He talked with a recruit who looked to be about sixteen.

"You are fighting for Palestine," he began. "But what kind of Palestine? And what would you do with the Jews?"

The boy's replies were prompt, and correct. "A Palestine for all of us—Arabs and Jews. We are not fighting the Jews but the Zionist state." . . .

"What do you think of President Nasser?" "He let the Israelis fool him, but he is an honest man."

"What of King Hussein?" "He is an agent of the imperialists —like Israel."

This youthful commando recruit had offered two answers— one already a fact and one prophetic. Al Fatah's program did indeed propose a new Palestinian state in which both Arab and Jew could live together in peace, as Arabs and Jews had lived for many hundreds of years before the Balfour Declaration.[9] And King Hussein began to demonstrate all too soon that he was more concerned with his own skin and throne than with the welfare of his Palestinian subjects. In 1970 he would collaborate with Israel and the United States in a deliberate attempt to crush the Palestine Liberation Movement.

The commandos of Al Fatah considered themselves freedom fighters—Fedayeen, those who sacrifice themselves. To their enemies at Amman, Tell Aviv, and Washington they were terrorists.

Al Fatah adopted some of the ideas and practices of the Algerian revolutionaries of 1954–62. It believed with the late Franz Fanon that for the oppressed, violence restores self-respect.

Yasir Arafat was born in Jerusalem in 1929. After the 1948 fighting he went to Cairo and won an engineering degree at King Fuad University, now the University of Cairo. There he became an authority on explosives and returned to Gaza to make use of his knowledge. After the Suez affair in 1956 he organized Al Fatah as a wholly Palestinian movement.

In the months after the 1967 debacle the various Palestinian resistance groups went each its own way. The personal ambitions of rival leaders and, especially in the case of the PFLP, vigorous ideological differences blocked efforts at united action until on February 1, 1969, a new 105-member Palestine Council convened at Cairo. With President Nasser prodding them, the leaders of fourteen resistance organizations agreed to combine their efforts under a single new Palestine Liberation Organization with Al Fatah's Arafat in command. Nasser turned over to the new unit what was left of the original PLO, some seven thousand men.

Arabs and the Resistance   The pro-Zionism of American news was nowhere better illustrated than in the fog of confusion that surrounded resports of Palestinian commando operations. Israelis referred to raids and attacks by somebody called simply Arabs and used that generic term to justify bombing and shelling towns and villages wherever it seemed to offer them some immediate advantage. United States newsmen adopted the Israeli line and reported that "Arabs" had ambushed on Israeli patrol, raided an Israeli settlement, or blown up a pumping station. When Al Fatah guerillas set fire to an oil refinery at Haifa, that, too was the work of "Arabs."[10] Israel used the term expressly to subordinate and conceal the activities and effectiveness of the Palestinian resistance. Television and the press adopted the practice, largely because "Arabs" rolled more easily off announcers' tongues and fit more readily into headlines than "Palestinians" and "liberation organizations."

Indeed, Prime Minister Golda Meir argued that there was no such national entity as a Palestinian people, and the United States government said nothing to indicate its awareness of a Palestinian problem.

For Palestinian refugees, however, belief in their status as a people had been an article of faith translated into action.

Yasir Arafat explained in an interview in 1969:

Ever since 1948 the cry of more than a million Palestinians has echoed through the Middle East. The Arab countries could do very little for them, even if they had tried, which they did not. . . .

When, after 1967, the Palestinians formed their guerilla groups and began their own campaign against Israel, they immediately struck a very responsive chord within the Arab psyche. All the guilt and shame of 20 years came pouring out in the form of support for the Palestinians.[11]

The commandos had little trouble getting recruits and money. Men came from all over the Arab world to enlist under Palestinian banners. A Foreign Legion composed chiefly of westerners entered Al Fatah's service. The nucleus of this new formation included four Americans, thirty Britons (of whom ten were women), twenty Irish, twenty French, ten West Germans, and eight Swedes. Among the others were men from Netherlands, Italy, various countries of eastern Europe, India, Guyana, and Guinea.[12]

Toward the Future The Palestinian struggle for liberation did not immediately achieve great successes. Guerilla war is a slow and painful process of attrition, and those who sneered at the Palestinians' painful progress ignored all the lessons of history. Algeria's ten million people took seven years to drive out the French. In the Aden region local patriots fought against seemingly hopeless odds year after year before Great Britain was forced to strike her colors there. In Vietnam the Viet Minh and the Viet Cong for more than two decades conducted guerilla operations first against the French, then against an autocratic regime in Saigon, and finally against the Americans. A people fighting for its right to live free and unoppressed does not weary of the struggle. When fathers fall or grow too old to fight, sons take up the battle.

One U.S. newswoman wrote:

It's the saddest sight in the Middle East to see these children

*from 6 to 14 jumping over hurdles and taking guns apart and
marching wide-eyed around the field. As the instructor shouts
"Forward!" the boys shout in reply "To Palestine!"*[13]

But these young boys and their parents saw nothing sad in
their experience. They were simply preparing themselves for the
tasks that lay ahead, as a young man studies law or medicine or
accounting. Their military training was only part of their
preparation. They went to school, too, in classes conducted
usually by women who had studied at colleges and universities
both in the Arab world and outside it. Female volunteers of all
ages cooked and cleaned and rolled bandages in the training
camps and did all the other jobs for which they were fitted.

The Palestinians were at war. They understood that their war
could be a long and painful one, but their hearts were in it and
they did not flinch. Some day—whenever that day might come—
they were going "home."

Palestine and the Arab States　　　　Several separate wars raged in
the Arab world, each distinct in goals and methods, although
ultimately all were part of the same weave. Men and their
leaders sometimes found themselves at cross purposes with one
or more of the other struggles. Established states concerned
primarily with the general war against Israel did not seek
the same objectives as the advocates of Arab revolution. The
Soviet Union and the United States, involved in their own contest for primacy in the Arab regions, were likely to differ from
their proteges on the course to be adopted. None of these other
groups could serve its own ends and stand always steadfast for
the rights and claims of the Palestinians.

Lebanese and Jordanian rulers resented and feared the presence of Palestinian commando forces and training camps inside
their territories because that invited Israeli retaliation such as
the raid on Beirut airport and the armored attack at Es Samu.
Both Jordan and Lebanon resorted to arms in attempts to rid

themselves of the Palestinians. King Hussein of Jordan had the added incentive that his artificial kingdom was historically and geographically an integral part of Palestine*; a Palestinian victory would almost certainly end his dynasty and perhaps his life. He collaborated almost eagerly with both the United States and Israel to protect himself.

Egyptian leaders sought a peace that would give them back Sinai and the Suez Canal. They continued to offer lip service to the rights and claims of the Palestinians, but it seemed unrealistic to believe that they would insist upon the accomplishment of Palestinian purposes at the cost of their own objectives. In 1971 President Anwar Sadat was willing to accept Israel's right to peaceful existence within secure boundaries—but the mere fact of Israel's continuing existence as a Zionist state would be a total defeat for the Palestinians.

Several wars in the Arab world continued. Not the least of these was the war waged by the Palestine Liberation Movement for a secular, binational state in what was once Palestine to which the Arab Palestinians could return.

* See note on page 23.

million metric tons. Half of the world's production was concentrated in Iran and the Arab world. Kuwait alone shipped 170 million tons of petroleum and Saudi Arabia 156 million in 1966.

The United States took a small part of this production for its own use in order to conserve its domestic reserves. Japan filled ninety-two percent of her oil needs with supplies from the Arab world. China, Australia, New Zealand, and most of Africa also went to the Arabs for petroleum. But most Arab production continued to move to western Europe.[5]

There's Money in Those Wells!   Producing, refining, and selling Arab oil assured rich profits. Arab petroleum was of very high quality. Its sulphur content was extremely low (as contrasted with that of oil from Venezuela, where sulphur content was very high). Kuwaiti oil cost 6.7 cents per barrel to produce in 1967 and the average for all Arab states was 15 cents. Venezuelan oil cost 51 cents and the Indonesian product 82 cents. United States production costs came to $1.15. These costs were certain to rise substantially after Iran and the gulf states negotiated new royalty agreements in 1970—but in an era of inflation American production costs were increasing, too.

United States companies exploiting Arab oil made a net profit of 81 cents per barrel in 1966. Statistical analysts Standard & Poor reported June 5, 1967, that Standard Oil (California) derived 36 percent of its 1966 income from Arab wells. Mobil Oil drew 25 percent of its income from the Arab world, Royal Dutch Shell 22 percent, Texaco 16, Standard Oil of New Jersey 15.6, and Gulf Oil 15 percent.[6] Ironically, the Standard & Poor analysis was released at the very moment when Israel was launching an attack on her Arab neighbors, Gamal Abdul Nasser was blocking the Suez Canal again, and the costs of transporting Arab oil were taking a new jump. In 1970 Arab oil cost consumers $26.50 per barrel (estimated production cost 79 cents per barrel).

WHERE ARAB OIL MONEY GOES[7]

Based on 1970 selling price of $26.50 per barrel in Europe
Production cost estimated at 79 cents per barrel

Royalties and share of profit to producing states	$3.30
Transportation*	2.00
Refining*	4.20
Distribution*	6.00
Taxes in consuming countries	10.00
Reinvestment by companies	.40
Company dividends	.60

*Costs listed under these categories include the profits earned
by subsidiary companies to whom transportation, refining, and
distribution functions were assigned. The dividends listed are
only those paid by the parent company.

The oil companies published no clear statement of costs and
profits nor, in those figures that they did release, did they call
attention to the fact that their subsidiary corporations engaged
in transportation, refining, and marketing all skimmed off a
profit before the parent firms calculated earnings.

Clearly, any actual or threatened change in the political climate of the Arab world took on vast importance both at Washington and at London. (Britain's investment in Persian Gulf Oil,
almost all of it government owned, had risen from two million
pounds sterling in 1914 to more than a billion pounds sterling
in 1968.) In June 1967 when Kuwait and Iraq briefly shut off the
export of oil to the west and a general Arab oil embargo seemed
possible, the United States used every diplomatic and economic
weapon to defeat an Iraqi proposal for the nationalization of
natural resources by all Arab states. At that time the United
States still had power in Libya and Saudi Arabia. Britain still
had political power in Kuwait. Those three Arab governments
blocked adoption of Iraq's bold scheme.

Who Get's What?   Details of the arrangements through which foreign oil companies compensated Arab states and kept high profits for themselves do not lie within the scope of this report. Several competent works on the development and exploitation of Arab petroleum have already been published. We restrict ourselves to the political and economic role of oil in the Arab world.

Most contracts required payments of royalties, calculated as a percentage of oil produced. In practice, however, payment was made in money because the foreign companies owned the channels of transportation and sale. Royalties were therefore determined on the basis of posted prices at the ports of embarkation. The posted price was an arbitrary figure set by the firms themselves and represented far less than export petroleum was actually worth at the point of shipment. (A sharp increase in posted prices was one of the demands by the gulf states in bargaining at Tehran in 1971.) The margin between posted price and ultimate selling price was the companies' own concern.

In the beginning no Arab state owned refineries. They owned no tankers and had no marketing facilities. They had to sell their royalty oil as crude petroleum and their only customers were the people who owned the concessions in their territory. The companies earned big profits not only on their share of the oil but on the Arab states' royalty oil as well.

Whatever royalty payments the producing countries might extract from the western corporations, they got only a minor share of a vital product that began by being all theirs. Local taxes levied in some states and charges for essential services such as telephone and telegraph added a little to the host states' revenue. Wages paid to native labor or spent locally by foreigners entered the national economy, but the concessionaires still recovered far, far more than they ever expended. That, of course, is the essence of the private profit system.

Corporate profits were a return on investment. The capital itself remained intact. Each year accountants set aside reserves

from income for depreciation and maintenance (including allowances for the ultimate exhaustion of the wells) before profits
were calculated. United States investors in Arab oil made
another rich killing: what the companies and their friends in
Congress called a depletion allowance. This charge against
income had already been taken into careful account on the
firms' own books; now it was figured again under the law before
taxes were paid. Until 1969 the depletion allowance had been
set at 27½ percent of net income, but insistent congressmen
got it reduced to 20 percent—still a fat bonanza. In sober fact
the companies recovered their original investment many times
over while still keeping it whole.

The petroleum-producing countries had no such protection.
They were in just such a position as one who inherits a great
fortune in collected works of art and lives by selling off his
treasures one by one. Ultimately the hapless heir will have
nothing left to sell. The dealers who handled his art will shrug
him aside and look elsewhere for things to buy and to sell. The
owners of cut-over timber lands can stay in business with a
program of reforestation, but noboby has developed a way to
refill exhausted oil wells.

Nationalization   When Premier Mustafa Mossadegh took
over Iran's oil and tried to exploit it for the benefit of the state,
he failed. Every western country collaborated with Britain
against him. They pumped a little more oil in other regions to
make up for the loss of Iranian petroleum and closed every
western market against Iranian oil. They owned the world's
tanker fleets, almost all its refineries outside the communist
states, and all the marketing channels through which petroleum
products reached western buyers. In twenty-seven months Iran
sold just three cargoes of oil, to Italy and Japan.

More than seventy-five percent of the world's known oil
reserves lay in Iran and the Arab world. Indonesia and Vene-

zuela also had exportable surpluses, and some existed in the Caribbean. The United States could survive almost indefinitely on its own petroleum resources, but Europe, Asia, Africa, and the rest of the world had to look to the Arabs and Iranians, no matter who might own and run the oil business there.

Egypt's nationalization of the Suez Canal in 1956 illustrates this issue. After 1956 the ships of the world continued to use that waterway because it served their needs, and the fact that Egypt—not an Anglo-French corporation—operated the canal and collected income from it concerned canal users not at all. So it would be if and when Arab states decided to take over the production, processing, transportation, and distribution of their own petroleum in their own behalf.

In the years after 1956—and particularly after 1967—the situation favored nationalization. A Soviet naval force patrolled the eastern Mediterranean. Other Soviet units operated in the Indian Ocean. Arab states opened their harbors to supply and service those ships. Western countries no longer ruled the world's tanker fleets. Japan, the USSR, and some Arab countries already owned such vessels, capable of moving large quantities of oil, and more were being built.

Several Arab states had new, modern refineries. South Yemen had at Aden the largest refining and petrochemical research facility in the world. Engineers and technicians from the Soviet bloc and within the Arab lands themselves deprived the west of its former monopoly on needed knowledge and skills.

Oil and Strategy   In March 1971 a new coalition, the Organization of Petroleum Exporting Countries, acted to buy and build tankers, acquire additional refineries, and set up a marketing system that would concentrate at first on the traditional European market and spread in time to every region compelled to import petroleum. OPEC included the Persian Gulf states of Iran, Iraq, Saudi Arabia, Kuwait, Qatar, and Abu Dhabi (of these five are Arab) plus Algeria, Libya, Venezuela, Indonesia, and Nigeria (of these two are Arab and two are Muslim, sympathizing with the Arabs).

To compensate for the devaluation of the dollar in December 1971 OPEC countries asked for $400 million more on their current contract and $75 million per month in the future. Meanwhile, the Arab states were requesting an agreement whereby they would have the right to buy out their oil contracts, the purpose being to bring pressure on the oil companies.

When—no longer if!—the Arab world assumed total ownership and control of its oil resources, the western nations would have two alternatives, accept Arab nationalization or try to use military force to prevent it. The Suez folly of 1956 and the USSR's commitment to the Arab countries make military resistance to nationalization virtually unthinkable.

Few know that the strength of American oil companies lies not in that black gold but rather in the conventional gold. By controlling production they have accumulated huge amounts in cash reserves, used for collateral investments in related industries likely to help them maintain the political control so necessary to operation. Short of nationalization the oil-producing Arab states can force these companies to use their enormous political influence to counterbalance Zionist influence. Arab revolutionary governments have not yet done this but would make it their first step before nationalization. If Arab oil produces cash reserves, these should benefit Arabs.

Russia would not divert oil from Europe, as will be discussed in chapter 34, but will actively work at divesting that oil of American control.

32: WATER

Desperate problem in a thirsty region

NOWHERE is the need for more fresh water greater than in some of the Arab lands. This is especially true in Jordan and the rest of Palestine, where the Jordan River is the only large stream. The Jordan starts its troubled journey high in Syria's Anti-Lebanon mountains. In Palestine just below the borders of Syria and Lebanon, a broad, deep depression provides a natural reservoir. Men once called it the Sea of Galilee. Today it is Lake Tiberias. Beyond Tiberias the Jordan renews its travel to the Dead Sea, on whose shores Sodom and Gomorra stood.

The Hasbani River runs down out of Lebanon to feed the Jordan. From Syria come the Dan and the Banias. Most of the Jordan River's valley lies east of the stream inside the kingdom of Jordan. At no point inside Israel's 1949 boundaries is the valley more than thirty miles wide; and on this fact of geography hinges much of the bitter dispute over use of the Jordan River's flow.

Men have lived here for many thousands of years. King Solomon had brass foundries here. Ancient tribes used the valley clay to make bricks. Bridges carried caravans out of Palestine toward Damascus and Byzantium. Camel trains from Saba—or Sheba—in Yemen passed this way, and scholars speculate that the Arab Queen of Sheba was in Jerusalem to negotiate transit rights through this valley when she visited Solomon. Their son,

323

as Menelik I, founded the dynasty that still rules Ethiopia.

The river has always provided a natural boundary between the eastern and western regions of Palestine. When Britain divided Palestine to serve her own politico-military interests and block the spread of Zionism through that territory, she chose the river to be a boundary between Transjordan and the rest of the country.

The Jewish Agency for Palestine soon after its establishment set engineers to plan the Jordan's flow for the Zionists' sole use. Not until 1939, however, when the Zionist determination to create a sovereign Jewish state could no longer be concealed from the world, was the scheme made known. In that year an American, Walter Lowdermilk, outlined for the Agency a water diversion plan calculated to sustain a population of as many as six million in a Jewish Palestine, but while Britain ruled that region the Lowdermilk scheme remained that and nothing more.

In 1948 Transjordan's Arab Legion seized Samaria, Judea, and the northern Negev. But Israel ruled the southern shore of Lake Tiberias, and in 1953 she began to carry out the Lowdermilk plan. Syria protested to the Mixed Armistice Commission and General Odd Bull, the chairman of that United Nations body, ordered the project scrapped. It violated the terms of the armistice, he ruled. From that moment forward Israel refused to participate in the commission or recognize its authority. Israel, we know from her unsavory record, has always refused to abide by any rule or agreement that challenged her own selfish interests.

The (Eric) Johnston Plan   U.S. Zionists demanded that Washington intervene to advance the Israeli claims, and in October 1953 Dulles sent Eric Johnston into the Arab world with what purported to be a new scheme for the mutual development of the Jordan's waters that would benefit all the affected states. Certainly it was not new, nor was the mutuality of its provisions visible.

Reporters dubbed this the Johnston Plan, although Eric Johnston was never more than an errand boy for Zionists and their political supporters. He was a former president of the United States Chamber of Commerce, highly paid czar of the Hollywood movie industry, and had been a lavish contributor to Republican campaign funds.

The so-called Johnston Plan had in fact been prepared by two engineers of the Tennessee Valley Authority, James B. Hays and J. V. Savage, it was nothing more nor less than a refurbished edition of the Lowdermilk proposal. Hays later explained the plan in detail.[1] The Zionist Dr. Emanuel Neumann declared in his introduction to the Hays book that the United Nation's 1947 partition plan "awarded [Israel] an area embracing the upper reaches of the Jordan . . . [She] was thereby given the opportunity of carrying out the conception of the Lowdermilk and Hays project."

According to another observer, Israel's purpose under the Hays program was simply to "take as much as possible of the Jordan's water right out of the Jordan's own valley, away from the people of it," and permit the development of new agricultural areas in the barren Negev desert one hundred and fifty miles away.[2]

The attempt to take the waters of the Jordan to support large numbers of new Jewish immigrants far outside the natural river basin roused inevitable opposition, not only in Jordan, Lebanon, and Syria but in every other Arab state. In 1951 a British engineering firm, Sir Murdoch Macdonald and Partners, had given the Jordanian government a plan to divide the flow between Jordan and Israel but without permitting any of that water to be carried beyond the limits of the river valley. He wrote:

The general principle, which to our mind has an undeniable moral and natural basis, [is] that the waters in a catchment area should not be diverted outside this area unless the requirements of all who use or genuinely intend to use the waters within the area have been satisfied.[3]

Water and the Law   The moral and natural principles proclaimed by Macdonald were also the basis of world law governing the riparian rights of states and individuals.

When California proposed to divert huge quantities of water from the mighty Colorado River to supply a growing population in her coastal area, every other state in the Colorado basin objected. Long years of litigation ended only when the U.S. Supreme Court made provision for satisfying the needs of the basin states and authorized California to take some of the surplus.

Wisconsin, Indiana, Michigan, and other states in the Great Lakes basin fought the plan of the city of Chicago to divert water from Lake Michigan to reverse the flow of the Chicago River, carry off effluent from Chicago's sewage disposal system, and provide a channel for barge traffic from the Mississippi. This issue, too, went to the Supreme Court, which set a precise limit on the quantities of lake water that Chicago could divert.

These disputes could be settled peaceably because every political unit affected was bound to the single legal system of one country. In the Jordan River controversy four sovereign nations claimed rights in the flow, and there was no central legal or judicial system with authority over their actions. Israel merely ignored the rule of law. National sovereignty, she argued, entitled her to do as she liked with waters inside her political boundaries.

No court in any land, however, had recognized the authority of any state to divert the waters of any body that touched the territories of other governments.[4] In 1907 the U.S. Supreme Court ordered Kansas to abandon a scheme for use of Arkansas River water to the detriment of other states farther downstream. In 1922 the Court ruled that Colorado could not divert the North Platte River to Wyoming's disadvantage. In 1927 in a dispute over the waters of the Danube German courts held that "no state has the right to cause substantial injury to another state by the use it makes of the water of a natural waterway." No court anywhere has ever ruled otherwise.

In August 1956 the International Law Association discussed the Jordan River problem and adopted the view that:

While each state has sovereign control over the rivers within its boundaries, the state must exercise this control with due consideration for its effect upon other riparian states . . . A state which proposes new works (diversion, construction, etc.) or changes of previously existing use which might affect utilization of the water by another state must first consult with the other state.

In 1958 the ILA concluded:

Except as provided by treaty or other instrument, or custom binding upon the parties, each coriparian state is entitled to a reasonable and equitable share in the use of the waters of the drainage basin. What amounts to a reasonable and equitable share is a question to be determined in the light of all relevant factors in each particular case.

Israel's planned diversion of the Jordan's flow seriously threatened agricultural development in the kingdom of Jordan, but the Zionist rulers at Tel Aviv shrugged the facts and the law aside. Confident that the world's greatest power, the United States, would protect her from retaliation, she plunged ahead with her program.

The Other Side of the Coin   Members of the Arab League decided to turn Israel's arguments against her. If she could do as she wished with the river where it passed through her territory, Syria and Lebanon could do the same with the Jordan's tributaries inside their borders. The gander proposed to feed on the sauce that the goose was claiming.

Syria began to dig, inside her own borders, a canal that would

divert the Banias River's flow out of the Jordan River system
into King Hussein's territory. Lebanon began work on a plan
to reverse the flow of the Hasbani River to keep its water inside
Lebanon and to draw off the waters of the Wazzani springs.
These schemes, carried to their conclusion, would make Lake
Tiberias little more than a mudhole. The Jordan, where it ran
through Israel, would be a dry and ugly wadi.

The claim of sovereign right lost its flavor in Israel and the
Zionist state turned to armed might again. "We cannot permit
a canal 50 miles long to be built under our noses," Prime
Minister Levi Eshkol warned.[5] "For us," he added, "the water
plan is of vital importance. Any attempt to obstruct the implementation of this plan will be considered an act of aggression
and dealt with accordingly."

On September 4, 1965, Israeli troops entered Jordan and
blew up eleven pumps supplying water for Jordanian farms.
On May 15, 1966, the *New York Times* reported that another
new Israeli pumping plant was already in use. Israel was taking
172 million gallons per day from the Jordan River system;
sixteen months earlier, the report pointed out, she had pledged
that she would not attempt to draw off more than 140 million
gallons.

On July 14, 1966, artillery and aircraft bombarded the Banias
canal project inside Syria. In the United Nations Security
Council six states voted for a resolution condemning this latest
Israeli aggression. No country voted or spoke against it, but
the resolution did not pass. Adoption required nine affirmative
votes. Britain, France, and the United States abstained and
rounded up six other abstainers to protect the Zionist government.

Salt and Pollution   Seepage from the Mediterranean fed bub-
bling springs in the bed of Lake Tiberias with ocean brine. This
process had been continuing for untold centuries and the water
of the lake was growing dangerously saline. Early in her water

development program Israel had drained the Huleh marshes upstream of Tiberias and laid out farms there. Any withdrawal of fresh water above the reservoir intensified the salt problem, and loss of the flow of the Huleh water, which once had fed the Jordan River system, had made the situation worse. Rainfall was always meager, and the system just did not receive enough fresh water to compensate for the saline increase.

Between 1960 and 1964 the salt content of Israel's irrigation water increased fifteen percent from 316 milligrams per cubic meter to 365. No one knew precisely how heavy the saline concentration would have to be to make agriculture impossible, but agronomists agreed that 365 milligrams was probably very near the tolerable limit. This created the possibility that whatever might happen in the military and political arena, nature itself could some day defeat Israel's grandiose irrigation scheme.

Man was contributing heavily to the danger, too. In Israel as in other lands where populations increased and industrial expansion flowered, human and industrial wastes were poisoning the water supply. Not until 1970 did this grave danger begin to be recognized in Israel, but at least it was tackled more vigorously and successfully than, for example, in the United States. There were no huge combines and lobbies to oppose or evade needed stringent controls, and the very meagerness of water sources in a time of political and military stress assured a greater public awareness and willingness to clean up the environment.

Ray of Hope   Every state in the Arab world has access to the oceans and seas, and throughout the world scientists and engineers are working on programs to make sea water generally usable by taking the salt out of it. The United States has maintained an Office of Saline Water since 1952 and has experimental desalting plants operating in Texas. Other bigger units are being built or are in the planning stage.

Several methods have been tried. Their aim is to evaporate sea brine, letting the salt precipitate out of it, and condense the salt-free water vapor for human use. In 1971 it was still impossible to produce potable water in quantities large enough for general use. Even the most economical methods yet devised produced fresh water at a minimum cost of forty cents per thousand gallons. The immediate goal was to cut that figure in half.

British engineers at Aden built the first feasible desalination plant in the Arab world in 1937. It had a capacity of four hundred thousand gallons per day. Various British and American firms later erected larger systems in Kuwait, Israel, and other countries.

It is possible—even, perhaps, probable—that man can some day soon eliminate the terrible shortage of water as a cause of new conflict in the Arab regions. Meanwhile, however, the desperate need for water continues to be a threat.

33: THE ARAB NATION AND THE ARAB REVOLUTION
Goal of a people

As FAR BACK as recorded history goes there are references to the Arabs as a separate people. At first the term was restricted to those living in the southern region of the Arabian peninsula, in what is now Yemen. Later the northern tribes were included.[1] The word Arab broadened in application from only the nomadic bedouin to embrace all those peoples who were or became integral members of the Arab community of language,* customs, and tradition.[2]

Language and tradition play vital roles in establishing and maintaining any national identity. Nuseibeh cites the common language as a primary factor in the development of an Arab national consciousness. Albert Hourani asserts:

The poems, traditions, and legends expressed in spoken literature and oral tradition . . . molded the minds of the Arabs, fixed their character, and made them morally and spiritually a nation before Muhammad welded the groups into a single organism animated by one purpose (Islam).[3]

* See note page 6.

331

Much of this has been discussed in chapter 1. Islam became the first truly unifying factor in Arab nationalism, and the acceptance of Islam by almost all Arab tribes produced the Islamic culture which left so strong an imprint not only on the Arab people but on all those who lived for centuries under its influence. This applies with special force to the Afro-Asian Jews who made their homes in Muslim—particularly the Arab—countries.

Islam is a body of doctrine based on the principle of Tawhid—"asserting oneness". It teaches that one god, Allah, is the source of all life, and it is a universal, not a tribal or national faith.[4] Its holy book, the Koran, is in Arabic. Its prophet was an Arab. He preached first to Arabs, and Arabs were the human agents through whom Islam reached the world beyond Arabia. Arabic thus became and has remained the classical language of theology and law among Muslims everywhere. These forces established the foundation of Islamic culture. The Jews and Christians who lived long in Islam came naturally under the powerful influence of that culture and became a part of it.

In vast regions conquered by Arab armies what Muhammad envisioned as an Islamic nation became in fact an Arab empire. It contributed much in science, literature, medicine, mathematics, and other fields of learning to the western world. Peoples of previously non-Arab lands were brought into the Arab nation and made full members of it.

The ethnic and cultural bonds that gave the Arabs of another age a consciousness of nationhood persisted through the centuries of their subjugation. Under Turks and Europeans they remained unconquerably Arab. The Zionist invasion of Palestine under British military protection reminded Arabs in every land of their basic oneness. When the events that followed World War II afforded them an opportunity to cast off the burden of foreign domination, they acted not solely as Syrians or Egyptians or Iraqis but once more, despite the passage of hundreds of years, as Arabs. Now they entered their revolutionary phase.

The Arab Revolution   Throughout, this study mentions the Arab revolution and outlines most of the conditions that produced it without trying to define or describe it. The omission was deliberate. The Arab revolution derives from the ethnic and cultural bonds of Arab history, from the Islamic civilization in which the Arab world attained a place of power and glory, and from the centuries in which Arab peoples lived, struggled, and survived under foreign rule.

The Arab revolution defies easy definition in orthodox terms. It cannot be described in Marxist jargon, nor can any clear analogy be made between this movement and the various revolutionary drives elsewhere. Nasser in Egypt and Ben Bella in Algeria argued that the Arab revolution is a product of Arab experience designed to serve Arab needs, and the observer is forced to accept their analysis.

The Russian revolution of 1917 rested upon a firm ideological base already laid by Karl Marx and V. I. Lenin. It was led by men schooled in a planned program of social, economic, and political thought. It sought to overthrow a native government with its own local support and its own ideological formula in a state that had maintained a national existence for centuries. The Russian revolution thus had none of the nationalistic character that made revolution in the Arab world possible. The Russian revolution with its call, "Workers of the world, unite!" was a direct denial of all nationalist theory.

In Russia, Russians, feudal lords, and kulaks owned the farmlands. In Egypt and Algeria most of the good land belonged to foreigners. The Russian revolution depended upon the disciplined support of an urban proletariat. In such states as Egypt and Algeria city workers were relatively few and wholly unorganized. Revolution in these countries drew its mass support from the rural areas. The Soviet Union undertook almost immediately to bring the agricultural lands under state control. Arab revolutionaries seized large estates and turned them over not to state agencies but to landless farmers.

Arab Socialism   The Arab revolution adopted a socialistic organization of industry and big business from need rather than preference. The western imperialists in the Arab world had seized control of the economic apparatus. To preserve their control they systematically prevented the development of a native class of executives, administrators, and technicians.

Economic mastery begets political domination in any state in any era. The revolutionaries' determination to destroy foreign ownership and management of the economy, in order to protect their new political grip, left their states with very few native citizens capable of operating the existing economy, and there was no alternative except total control by government. Nasser in Egypt and Ben Bella in Algeria began to build what they called Arab socialism because no other course lay open to them. The Syrian experience suggests that existence of a strong native middle class would have made a resort to some socialistic program inevitable in any event; in Syria the banker-merchant-clergy coalition resisted every attempt at political and economic change as long as it could, and only when that power that been smashed was it possible to introduce revolutionary programs. The Syrians resorted to socialistic doctrine, too, because they had to.

Again, it is important to note that Arab revolutionary leaders did not blindly follow the Soviet example in the development of their economy. If they adopted measures and policies similar to some of those used in the USSR, it was not because established socialist doctrine prescribed them, but because in various circumstances those policies and those measures seemed calculated to meet an immediate Arab need or serve an Arab purpose.

The new Arab socialism, for the most part, had no ideological foundation on which to build. No one has yet evolved a definitive theory of Arab revolution and Arab socialism. The revolution was and remains a pragmatic thing, subject to continuing review. In communist states leaders still quarrel fiercely over who and what does or does not accord with the Marxist-

Leninist line. In revolutionary Arab countries the application of socialistic remedies for local ills is a matter for each land to decide for itself. As the disastrous merger of Egypt and Syria showed, it is probably impossible to enforce in one national area the same ideas and schemes that have proved effective in another until and unless conditions in the one region approximate those in the other.

In Egypt, Iraq, and Algeria revolution began as a drive to destroy foreign rule and became a socio-economic struggle only after the outlanders had been expelled. Victory in the internal power contests then went to men bent on social change. If the United States in those years had been supporting the Arab states instead of Israel, it is altogether possible that control of the Cairo government might well have remained with a Naguib, not a Nasser. The Arab revolution might have taken an altogether different path.

The revolution did not spring full panoplied from the brow of some Jovian intellect. It moved step by hesitant step, retreating a little here, moving forward boldly there, testing methods, discarding plans that failed and pushing on with those that succeeded. Each new success provided a launching platform for the next leap forward.

Arab leaders wedded to old ways by their selfish interests or by conscious choice fought to stem the revolution. Rivalries between the protectors of the past and the advocates of a new Arab world reduced the League of Arab States to a condition of political paralysis, relieved only by its members' almost universal attachment to the idea of Arab nationhood and their implacable opposition to Zionist Israel.

The Nature of Revolution   Apologists for western rule in the Arab world made almost a liturgy of their claim that the western occupation brought local gains in health, civil administration, communications, and material assets, and their argument had just enough truth to make it plausible. They ignored the fact that imperial rulers and foreign entrepreneurs took far more than they gave.

Revolution breeds best where the fruits of progress and prosperity are most unfairly distributed. It is not in the nature of man to be content with the scraps dropped from another's table. In the Arab world western wealth stood forth on boastful display. Ruling whites took their indolent ease at the Turf Club or Shepherd's and the wheels of their carriages—then their cars —churned bitter dust for donkey drivers to plod through. Western films revealed such luxury as no ordinary Arab dreamed of. Even the common soldiers in white armies could hire native servants.

Few Arabs learned to read and write. They had no schools. Those who achieved a little learning had small hope of higher education. Those who earned degrees faced greater obstacles to worthy employment than United States blacks of sixty years ago. Resentment and bitterness grew and flowered not only in the minds of the poor unlettered but in those of the educated who knew more about the character of the world from which their oppressors had sprung.

Thomas Jefferson wrote in the United States Declaration of Independence:

> [A]ll experience hath shewn that mankind are more disposed to suffer, while evils are sufferable, than to right themselves by abolishing the forms to which they are accustomed. But when a long train of abuses and usurpations pursuing invariably the same Object, evinces a design to reduce them under an absolute Despotism, it is their right, it is their duty, to throw off such Government, and to provide new Guards for their security.

"Revolutions," Wendell Phillips commented, "are not made; they come. A revolution is as natural a growth as an oak. It comes out of the past. Its foundations are laid far back."

The foundations of the Arab revolution had been laid long since. Its genesis was in the national memory of a time when Arabs had been strong and powerful—and free. If there be

impertinent. Are they not the first revolutionaries of the modern world? Is not their Declaration of Independence a ringing revolutionary document for men of all ages to invoke in the name of freedom and equality?

They are indeed entitled to be proud. But recalling one's own revolution is perhaps not enough, or at least is a different thing from understanding another's hunger for revolutionary change. It becomes even less adequate when America's original revolution and its ideological underpinnings no longer seem relevant to the deep current of human events where men now need revolution most—among the masses of an emerging world.

Assessment of Revolutionary Progress   No leader or group, however, can make a revolution; they can only call attention to the need for it. Men resent the wrongs they suffer. They protest and demonstrate and fight. But the struggle becomes revolution only when nonrevolutionary methods fail. Revolution in Egypt began as a protest against royal incompetence and foreign rule. Revolution was possible only after the milk-and-honey remedies of a Naguib could not provide any improvement. Nasser, for all his skill and dedication, could not have led a revolution while hope remained that less drastic measures could meet Egypt's need. One step led to the next, and along the way the fight for a change became full fledged revolution. It would be difficult to say just when the Egyptian revolution really became a fact. The process began in 1919 when a popular rebellion led to an army coup d'etat. It moved forward with the failure of the Egyptian army in Palestine in 1948, and again when Gamal Abdul Nasser dumped Muhammad Naguib from the ruling junta in 1954. After that it merely crawled.

What might properly be called the people's revolution was yet to come. After Nasser won full power, he gathered a military elite that evolved into a military bureaucracy. He undertook and carried forward a considerable part of the social revolution he had preached, but what with the continuing battle against Israel and concern with maintaining his own power, the revolution seemed to bog down. Nasser's tremendous personal charisma won a fanatical popular devotion, even though most of the promises he made were not fulfilled. After his death Anwar Sadat's new regime was too busy cementing its domestic position and with the problems of the cease-fire program, so Egypt's revolutionary progress continued to lag. Following 1967 the Egyptian people slipped into a sort of apathetic lethargy in their attitude toward the war. They awaited and needed the internal spark of radical change. Sadat was not the one to provide it; he was a nationalist, not a revolutionist.

This did not mean Egyptians were any less determined nationalists, or that the Arab revolution concerned them less. Hostile new gestures from Israel would even then have brought instant action and eager support of whatever drastic measures the government might take, but it did mean that night club gaiety and a return to peace enchanted them more than patriotic parades and impassioned speeches. To many the bureaucratic new establishment differed all too little from the earlier one.

Algeria under Houari Boumedienne, on the other hand, moved into that second phase called the people's revolution. Under Ben Bella an establishment bureaucracy had taken form in Algeria as in Egypt. Boumedienne divested that bureaucracy of its power and led the country farther along the popular revolutionary road.

The Palestine Liberation Movement, which began with no clear ideological base beyond its demand for a free state delivered from Zionist control, had by 1970 become a genuine revolutionary organization, and its impact was felt in Jordan, Syria, and Lebanon.

The changes that had taken place in Egypt, Syria, Yemen, Iraq, South Yemen, Sudan, and Libya were part of one broadly based process. They could no more be looked upon as separate events than Eisenhower's invasion of Normandy in 1944 could be considered something wholly apart from Hitler's attack against Poland in 1939.

Some national leaders—Washington, Bolivar, Lenin, Mao—enter history as symbols of revolution. Others play vital roles in the early years of revolution yet draw little attention in later times. The world has already forgotten that the Spanish revolt in 1936 was initiated by a man named Sanjurjo. When he died in an airplane crash, Francisco Franco took his place, and today Franco is the worldwide symbol of that counterrevolution.

Gamal Abdul Nasser will go into the history of Egypt and the history of the Arab revolution as the charismatic hero of his time. Others are taking—have taken—his place, but their accomplishments will only dull the luster of his legend, never erase it.

As 1972 came around almost every Arab leader was marking time, and to many an observer it seemed that the Arab revolution was on the decline. But the revolution will go on. Revolutionary trends always do. Arab reactionary forces and imperial designs may delay but will not halt it. It will move forward at one point, falter a little at another, but will continue. The Arab people are inexorably in revolution. They will in time reach their goals. In the process they will discard the nationalistic movement programs and soft ways of later-day leaders. A new leadership will have to simply mobilize the popular masses in order to effect the radical transformation of Arab society. The model is more likely to be Mao's than any other even though the Arab people are not suited to its rigorous application and ideological framework. They would soften it with the humane touch of Arabic-Islamic culture.

As they reach revolutionary maturity, the Arabs are becoming more concerned with themselves than with Israel. With this change and Israel's concurrent transformation, the problems existing today will in time wither away even though new ones are generated.

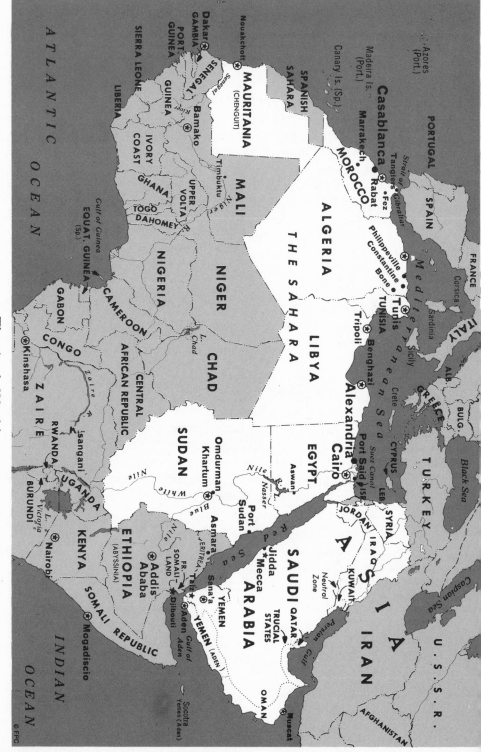

The Arab World

The Arabian Peninsula

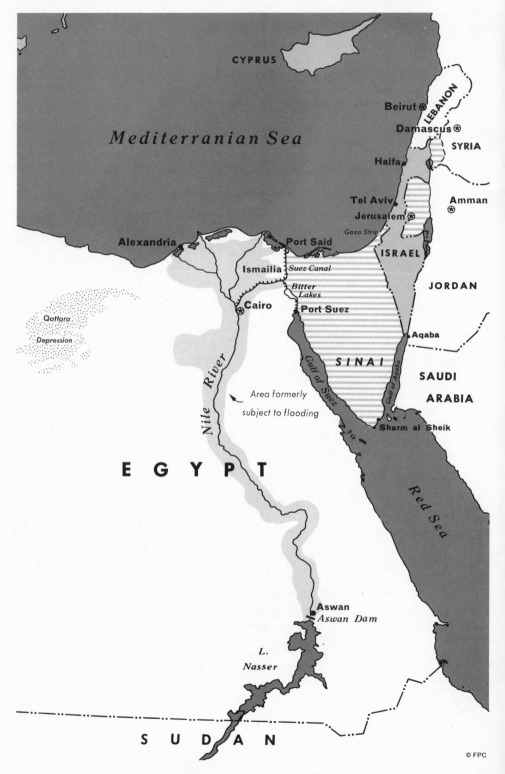

The Nile Valley and the Aswan High Dam

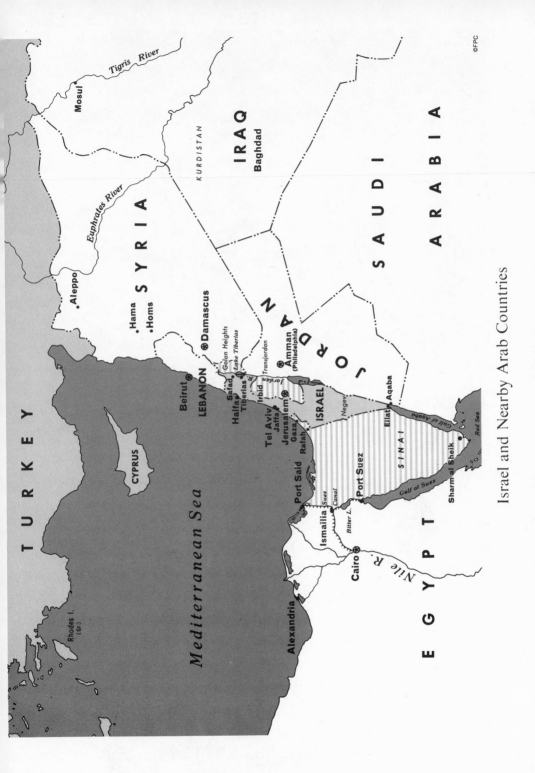

Israel and Nearby Arab Countries

Israel and Israel-Occupied Territories

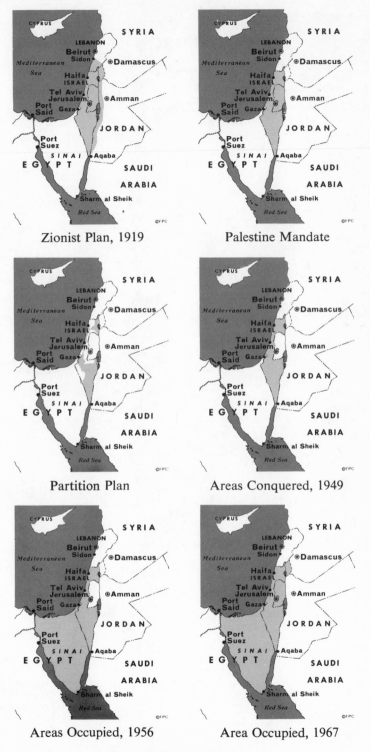

Zionist Plan, 1919

Palestine Mandate

Partition Plan

Areas Conquered, 1949

Areas Occupied, 1956

Area Occupied, 1967

Israeli Expansionism

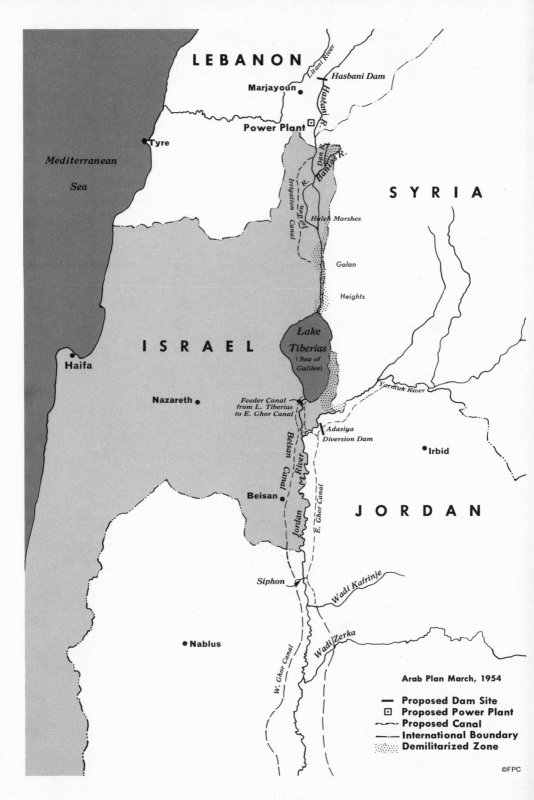

Jordon River Valley, Arab Plan

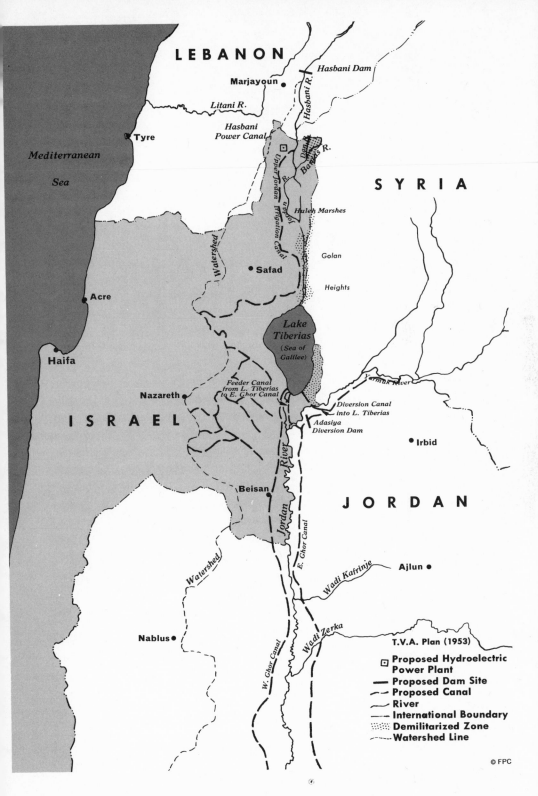

Jordan River Valley, T.V.A. Plan

NOTES

Chapter 1. THE ARABS: WHO THEY ARE AND WHENCE THEY CAME
1. Anthony Nutting, *The Arabs: A Narrative History* (New York: Potter, 1964), pp. 12–15; see also Philip Hitti, *History of the Arabs from the Earliest Times to the Present* (London: Macmillan, 1967).
2. Abd el Rahman Azzam, *The Eternal Message of Muhammad* (New York: Penguin, 1964). See also M. Cherif Bassiouni, "*Islam: Concept, Law and World Habeas Corpus,*" *Rutgers-Camden Law Journal* 1, no. 2 (Fall 1969):160–201.

Chapter 2. THE JEWS: A LOOK AT THEIR BEGINNINGS AND THEIR HISTORY
1. D. M. Dunlop, *The History of the Jewish Khazars* (Princeton: Princeton University Press, 1954). For a contrary position see Semen M. Dubnov, *History of the Jews in Russia and Poland*, vol. 1 (Philadelphia: Jewish Publication Society, 1916) and e.g., Abba Eban, *My People: The Story of the Jews* (New York: Random House, 1968).
2. Leon D. Epstein, *British Politics in the Suez Crisis* (Urbana: University of Illinois Press, 1964), pp. 180–5; see also Thomas Mallison, "*Legal Problems concerning the Juridical Status and Political Activities of the Zionist Organization; Jewish Agency: A Study of International and United States Law,*" *William and Mary Law Review*, 9(1968): 528–629.
3. Leonard Stein, *The Balfour Declaration*, app. 4 (London: Vallentine, 1961). For a history of Zionism see Israel Cohen, *The Zionist Movement* (London: Muller, 1945); Ben Halpern, *The Idea of the Jewish State* (Cambridge, Mass.: Harvard University Press, 1961); Arthur Herzberg, ed., *The Zionist Idea: A Historical Analysis and Reader* (New York: Greenwood, 1960); Chaim Weizmann, *Trial and Error: The Autobiography of Chaim Weizmann* (Philadelphia: Jewish Publication Society, 1949); *Encyclopedia of Zionism and Israel*, Raphael Patai, ed. (New York: McGraw-Hill, 1971).

Chapter 3. THE MANDATES: EUROPE IN THE ARAB WORLD
1. Thomas Mallison, "The Balfour Declaration: An Appraisal in International Law," in *The Transformation of Palestine*, ed. Ibrahim Abu-Lughod (Evanston, Ill.: Northwestern University Press, 1971), pp. 61–111; Walid Khalidi, *From Heaven to Conquest* (Beirut: Institute for Palestine Studies, 1971).
2. Paul L. Hanna, *British Policy in Palestine* (Washington, D.C.: American Council on Public Affairs, 1942); John Marlowe, *The Seat of Pilate: An Account of the Palestine Mandate* (London: Cresset, 1959); Christopher Sykes, *Crossroads to Israel* (London: Collins, 1965).
3. Anthony Nutting, *The Arabs: A Narrative History* (New York: Potter, 1964), chap. 25.
4. Fred J. Khouri, *The Arab-Israeli Dilemma* (Syracuse: Syracuse University Press, 1968), pp. 8–9.
5. Leonard Stein, *The Balfour Declaration*, app. 4 (London: Vallentine, 1961); Mallison, *The Balfour Declaration*.
6. Cherif Bassiouni, " 'Self-determination' and the Palestinians," *Proceedings of the American Society of International Law* (1971), p. 31.

Chapter 4. PALESTINE AND THE ZIONISTS:
BEGINNINGS OF CONFLICT
1. Great Britain, Palestine, Parliamentary Papers Cmd. 1700, (1922). See also Walid Khalidi, *From Heaven to Conquest* (Beirut: Institute for Palestine Studies, 1971); Thomas Mallison, "The Balfour Declaration: An Appraisal in International Law," in *The Transformation of Palestine*, ed. Ibrahim Abu-Lughod (Evanston: Northwestern University Press, 1971), pp. 61–111; Fred J. Khouri, *The Arab-Israeli Dilemma*, (Syracuse: Syracuse University Press, 1968), pp. 23–24. For documentation on this subject see E. L. Woodward, and R. Butler, eds., *Documents on British Foreign Policy, 1919–1939* (London: HMS, 1952).
2. Khouri, *Arab-Israeli Dilemma*, pp. 26–27.

Chapter 5. WORLD WAR II: WHAT IT MEANT TO THE ARABS
1. Samuel Halperin, *The Political World of American Zionism* (Detroit: Wayne State University Press, 1961); Nadav Safran, *The United States and Israel* (Cambridge, Mass.: Harvard University Press, 1963); Ibrahim Abu-Lughod, *Israel's Arab Policy*, and Kamel S. Abu-Jaber, *United States Policy Toward the June Conflict*, in *The Arab-Israeli Confrontation of June 1967*, ed. Ibrahim Abu-Lughod (Evanston, Ill: Northwestern University Press, 1970).

Chapter 6. ISRAEL: BIRTH OF AN ALIEN STATE
1. Dean Acheson, *Present at the Creation* (New York: Norton, 1970).
2. U.N. General Assembly Resolution 181 (xi), 29 November 1947.

3. M. Cherif Bassiouni, "*Some Legal Aspects of the Arab-Israeli Conflict,*" *Arab World*, 14(1968):79.
4. These figures are based on British estimates in E. L. Woodward and R. Butler, eds., *Documents on British Foreign Policy, 1919–1939* (London: HMS, 1952). For more recent statistics see Janet Abu-Lughod, "The Demographic Transformation of Palestine" in *The Transformation of Palestine*, ed. Ibrahim Abu-Lughod (Evanston, Ill.: Northwestern University Press, 1971).
5. Sumner Welles, *We Need Not Fail* (Boston: Houghton Mifflin, 1948); see also Fred J. Khouri, *The Arab-Israeli Dilemma* (Syracuse: Syracuse University Press, 1968), pp. 50–56.
6. James Forrestal, *Diaries*, ed. Walter Millis (New York: Viking, 1951), p. 363.

Chapter 7. THE PALESTINIAN DIASPORA:
THE FATE OF THE FIRST MILLION REFUGEES

1. John B. Glubb, *A Soldier with the Arabs* (New York: Harper, 1957), p. 81.
2. Arnold Toynbee, *A Study of History* (London: Oxford, 1935–54), 8:290.
3. Jon Kimche, *The Seven Fallen Pillars: The Middle East, 1945–1952* (New York: Praeger, 1953), p. 228.
4. John H. Davis, *The Evasive Peace* (London: Murray, 1968). Dr. Davis was a former Commissioner General of UNRWA.
5. U.N. General Assembly Resolution 194 (1948). See also M. Cherif Bassiouni, "Some Legal Aspects of the Arab-Israeli Conflict," *Arab World*, 14(1968):79 and M. Cherif Bassiouni, "The Palestinians: Refugees or a People?" *Catholic World*, September 1970.
6. Chesley Manley in *Chicago Tribune*, 26 September 1965.
7. Thomas F. Brady, "Arab Refugees Long for Their Home," *New York Times*, 21 March 1966.
8. Abba Eban, "The Arab Refugees," *Foreign Affairs*, April 1963. See also Don Peretz, "The Arab Peoples: A Changing Problem," *Foreign Affairs*, 41(April 1963):558–70.

Chapter 8. THE MAKING OF THE SUEZ CANAL
1. The reader who may be interested in the sordid, complex history of the building of the Suez Canal will find a wealth of detail in John Marlowe, *World Ditch: The Making of the Suez Canal* (New York: Macmillan, 1964), and Kenneth Love, *Suez: The Twice-Fought War* (New York: McGraw-Hill, 1969).

Chapter 9. EGYPT IN REVOLUTION:
THE DEATH KNELL OF IMPERIALISM

1. John Kenneth Galbraith, in *New York Times Magazine*, 5 January 1967.

2. Anwar Sadat, *Revolt on the Nile* (London: Wingate, 1957); Mohammed Naguib, *Egypt's Destiny* (London: Gollancz, 1955); Jean
LaCouture and Simonne LaCouture, *Egypt in Transition* (London:
Methuen, 1958).
3. Gamal Abdel Nasser, *The Philosophy of the Revolution* (Cairo: Mon-
diale Press, 195–, also published in the United States in 1955). See
also Charles D. Cremeans, *The Arabs and the World: Nasser's Arab
Nationalist Policy* (New York: Praeger, 1963) and Mohammed
Heikal, *Biography of Gamal Abdel Nasser* (New York: Doubleday,
1963). For a critical evaluation, see Anouar Abdel-Malek, *Egypt:
Military Society* (New York: Random House, 1968).

Chapter 10. THE ASWAN HIGH DAM: A TALE OF DULLES' FOLLY
1. "Aswan", *The Arab-Review*, special issue, (National Publications,
Cairo, 1964); Tom Little, *High Dam at Aswan* (London: Methuen,
1965).
2. Andrew Berding, *Dulles on Diplomacy* (Princeton: Van Nostrand,
1965).
3. Herman Finer, *Dulles Over Suez* (Chicago: Quadrangle Books, 1964),
p. 187.

Chapter 11. SUEZ 1956: IMPERIALISM REPULSED
1. M. Cherif Bassiouni, "The Nationalization of the Suez Canal,"
DePaul Law Review, 4, no. 2 (1965):258–98.
2. *Ibid.*
3. Kenneth Love, *Suez: The Twice-Fought War* (New York: McGraw-
Hill, 1969).
4. Hugh Thomas, *Suez* (New York: Harper, 1966), p. 65.
5. Bulganin's letters to Eden and Mollet are presented in full in Thomas,
Suez.
6. *Pravda* (Moscow), 23 August 1967, printed this statement in full; see
also Dmitrii T. Shepilov, *The Suez Problem* (Moscow, 1956).
7. Herman Finer, *Dulles Over Suez* (Chicago: Quadrangle Books, 1964),
pp. 328, 329.
8. Winthrop W. Aldrich, "The Suez Crisis," *Foreign Affairs*, 45(April
1967):541–52.
9. *Ibid.*
10. George W. Stocking, *Middle East Oil* (Nashville: Vanderbilt University
Press, 1970), pp. 152–8. For the impact of the Suez crisis on Europe
as well as an insight into its development see Anthony Nutting, *No
End of a Lesson: The Inside Story of the Suez Crisis* (New York:
Potter, 1967).

Chapter 12. JORDAN: AN UNEASY CROWN
1. Fred J. Khouri, *The Arab-Israeli Dilemma* (Syracuse: Syracuse University Press, 1968), p. 16.

2. William Yale, *The Near-East* (Ann Arbor: University of Michigan Press, 1958), pp. 382–4.
3. Khouri, *Arab-Israeli Dilemma*, pp. 187–8.
4. Thomas F. Brady in *New York Times*, 15 December 1966.
5. Hussein, King of Jordan, *Uneasy Lies the Head* (London: Heinemann, 1962); John B. Glubb, *A Soldier with the Arabs* (New York: Harper, 1957).

Chapter 13. SYRIA: THE OLD AND THE NEW IN CONFLICT
1. George Lenczowski, *The Middle East in World Affairs* (Ithaca: Cornell University Press, 1962). See also Abdul Latif Tibawi, *A Modern History of Syria Including Lebanon and Palestine* (New York: St. Martins, 1969); Kamel S. Abu-Jaber, *The Arab Ba'th Socialist Party: History, Ideology, and Organization* (Syracuse: Syracuse University Press, 1966).
2. Hisham B. Sharabi, *Governments and Politics of the Middle East in the Twentieth Century* (Princeton: Van Nostrand, 1962). See also Patrick Seale, *The Struggle for Syria: A Study of Post-War Arab Politics* (New York: Oxford, 1965).
3. George Antonius, *The Arab Awakening* (Toronto: Lippincott, 1939); Albert H. Hourani, *Arabic Thought in the Liberal Age: 1789–1939* (London: Oxford, 1962); George Lenczowksi, "Radical Regimes in Egypt, Syria and Iraq: Some Comparative Observations on Ideologies and Practices," *Journal of Politics*, 29(February 1966):29–56.
4. Hisham B. Sharabi, *Nationalism and Revolution in the Arab World.* (Princeton: Van Nostrand, 1966).
5. Charles Yost, "The Arab-Israeli War: How It Began," *Foreign Affairs*, 46(January 1968):304–20.

Chapter 14. IRAQ: DEATH OF A MONARCHY
1. Peter M. Holt, *Egypt and the Fertile Crescent, 1516–1922* (New York: Longmans, 1966).
2. Hisham B. Sharabi, *Governments and Politics of the Middle East in the Twentieth Century* (Princeton: Van Nostrand, 1962); Benjamin Shwadran, *The Power Struggle in Iraq* (New York: Council for Middle Eastern Affairs Press, 1959).
3. The nationalization of Iranian oil and its impact upon the nationalization program in Arab countries are discussed in a later chapter. See also George W. Stocking, *Middle East Oil* (Nashville: Vanderbilt University Press, 1970), pp. 152–8.
4. Elias Hoff, "The Baghdad Pact and Its Effect on the Arab States," (American University, thesis, Beirut, 1967).

Chapter 15. LEBANON: EXPERIMENT IN TOLERANCE
1. Abdul Latif Tibawi, *A Modern History of Syria Including Lebanon and Palestine* (New York: St. Martins, 1969); Leonard Binder, ed., *Politics in Lebanon* (New York: Wiley, 1966).

Chapter 16. ALGERIAN ALGERIA: REVOLUTION IN THE MAGHREB
1. U.S. Office of Education, *Educational Data: Algeria* (Washington: G.P.O., 1964).
2. *Ibid;* also Yves LaCoste, André Nouschi, and André Prenant, eds., *L'Algérie Passé et Présente* (Paris: Editions Sociales, 1960).
3. See *Record*, special issue on Algeria, vol. 1, no. 8 (New York: Keynote, 1963).
4. Arnold Mandel, "France's Algerian Jews," *Commentary*, June 1963.
5. William R. Polk, "The Nature of Modernization: The Middle East and North Africa," *Foreign Affairs*, 44(October 1965):100–10.
6. Manfred Halpern, *The Politics of Social Change in the Middle East and North Africa* (Princeton: Princeton University Press, 1963).

Chapter 17. MOROCCO: A KING AS NATIONALIST?
1. "Morocco: The St. Germain Caper," *Newsweek*, 15 November 1965, p. 61, and "Morocco: Shaking the Throne," *Newsweek*, 29 November 1965, p. 39.
2. Bernard Peyrouton, *Histoire Générale du Maghreb* (Paris: Michel, 1966); Manfred Halpern, *The Politics of Social Change in the Middle East and North Africa* (Princeton: Princeton University Press, 1963).
3. "Morocco: Hassan's Last Hurrah?" *Newsweek*, 6 December 1971.

Chapter 18. TUNISIA AND HABIB BOURGUIBA:
A NATION'S TALE AND A PERSONAL STORY
1. Bernard Peyrouton, *Histoire Générale du Maghreb* (Paris: Michel, 1966); Manfred Halpern, *The Politics of Social Change in the Middle East and North Africa* (Princeton: Princeton University Press, 1963).
2. "Tunisia," *Newsweek*, 10 May 1965, p. 50; *Manchester Weekly Guardian*, 13 May 1965.
3. *New York Times*, 28 May 1965.
4. *Ibid.*, 21 December 1965.
5. *Ibid.*, 11 February 1970.

Chapter 19. SUDAN: MOVING INTO REVOLUTION
1. Jacob C. Hurewitz, *Middle East Politics: The Military Dimension* (New York: Praeger, 1969), pp. 163–77.

Chapter 20. LIBYA: IMPERIAL SCHEMES, ARAB OIL, AND REVOLUTION
1. Majid Khadduri, *Modern Libya, A Study in Political Development* (Baltimore: Johns Hopkins Press, 1963).

Chapter 21. YEMEN: LAND OF THE QUEEN OF SHEBA
1. Anthony Nutting, *The Arabs: A Narrative History* (New York: Potter, 1964), ch. 7.
2. *New York Times*, 20 September 1962.
3. *Manchester Guardian Weekly*, 12 November 1964.

4. "The Yemen: A State in Progress," *Arab World*, April-May 1967.
5. *New York Times*, 31 August 1967.

Chapter 22. SAUDI ARABIA AND IBN SAUD:
THE OIL AND DESERT KINGDOM
[No notes.]

Chapter 23. AROUND THE RIM OF ARABIA:
OF OIL AND POLITICS
1. Sir Charles Johnston, *The View from Steamer Point* (London: Collins, 1964).
2. *Manchester Guardian Weekly*, 25 June 1964.
3. *Ibid.*, 19 July 1964.
4. Johnston, *View*.
5. James Morris, "Sundown at Aden," *Manchester Guardian Weekly*, 31 March 1966.
6. *Manchester Guardian Weekly*, 7 September 1967.
7. *Ibid.*, 23 November 1967.
8. *Chicago Sun-Times*, 8 December 1971.

Chapter 24. INSIDE ISRAEL: A NATION DIVIDED
1. Hugh Trevor-Roper, "Jewish and Other Nationalisms, *Commentary*, January 1963, p. 15.
2. *Newsweek*, 9 May 1966. See also "Israelis Repatriating Majorca's 'Catholic' Jews," *New York Times*, 3 October 1966.
3. J. Robert Moskin, "Prejudice in Israel," *Look*, 5 October 1965. See also *Zionism and the Arab Revolution: The Myth of Progressive Israel* (New York: Young Socialist Alliance, 1969).
4. Moskin, "Prejudice in Israel." See also *Zionism and the Arab Revolution*.
5. "Israel: The Search for Identity," *Newsweek*, 15 November 1965, p. 64.
6. Katznelson's book was never distributed in the United States. For a report of its content and political impact see "Israel: The Non-Europeans," *New Republic*, 2 May 1964, pp. 7–8. See in general Uri Avnery, *Israel Without Zionists* (New York: Macmillan, 1968).
7. Don Cook, "Israel: The Trouble with Success," *Chicago Sun-Times*, 18, 1966. See in general Moshe Menuhin, *The Decadence of Judaism in Our Time* (New York: Exposition Press, 1965).
8. "Israel: The Not-So-Lost Tribe," *Newsweek*, 18 October 1971.

Chapter 25. WAR 1967: FROM THE STRAIT OF TIRAN TO THE GOLAN
HEIGHTS
1. *New York Times*, 26 and 30 January 1967; 17 February 1967. For a collection of articles see *The Arab-Israeli Confrontation of June 1967*. ed., Ibrahim Abu-Lughod (Evanston, Ill.: Northwestern University Press, 1969).

2. *New York Times*, 9 April 1967.
3. *Ibid.*, 11 May 1967.
4. *Ibid.*, 19 May 1967.
5. *Ibid.*, 23 May 1967.
6. *Ibid.*, 24 May 1967.
7. *Ibid.*, 25 and 28 May 1967; 28 June 1967.
8. M. Cherif Bassiouni and Eugene M. Fisher, "The Arab-Israel Conflict: Real and Apparent Issues," *St. John's Law Review*, 44, no. 3 (January 1970):299–365. See also M. Cherif Bassiouni, "The Middle-East in Transition: From War to War, A Proposed Solution," *The International Lawyer*, 4(1970):379; M. Cherif Bassiouni, *"The 'Middle East'*—The Misunderstood Conflict," *Kansas Law Review*, 19 (1971):373.
9. *New York Times*, 31 May 1967.
10. *Ibid.*, 30 May 1967; 2 June 1967.
11. *Ibid.*, 30 June 1967.
12. *Ibid.*, 10 June 1967; Eric Pace, "Cairo Diary," *New York Times Magazine*, 2 July 1967.
13. Pace, "Cairo Diary."
14. *New York Times*, 29 June 1967.
15. *Ibid.*, 2 July 1967.
16. *Ibid.*, 5 July 1967.
17. *Ibid.*, 23 November 1967.
18. See, e.g., Georges G. Corm, *Les Finances d'Israel* (Beirut: The Institute for Palestine Studies, n.d.); "Israel's Trade Deficit Soars due to Military Expenditures," *Action*, 12 August 1970.

Chapter 26. THE PALESTINIANS GO TO WAR:
REFUGEES TURN FEDAYEEN

1. M. Cherif Bassiouni, "The Palestinians: Refugees or a People?" *Catholic World*, September 1970; *The Palestinian Resistance to Israeli Occupation*, ed., Naseer Aruri (Wilmette, Ill.: Medina University Press International, 1971); Hisham B. Sharabi, *Palestine and Israel: The Lethal Dilemma* (New York: Pegasus, 1969).
2. Abba Eban, "The Arab Refugees," *Foreign Affairs*, April 1963.
3. Chesley Manley, in *Chicago Tribune*, 26 September 1965.
4. Thomas F. Brady, "Arab Refugees Long for Their Home," *New York Times*, 21 March 1966.
5. Ray Moseley, in *Chicago Tribune*, 16 July 1966.
6. *New York Times*, 13 June 1966.
7. James Feren, in *New York Times*, 26 June 1967.
8. Walter Schwarz, in *Manchester Guardian Weekly*, 20 February 1969.
9. *Free Palestine*, January 1969.
10. *Newsweek*, 7 July 1969.
11. Nizar Jwaideh, in *Chicago Sun-Times*, 3 December 1969.

ISRAEL

Avnery, Uri. *Israel Without Zionists.* New York: Macmillan, 1968.

Fein, Leonard J. *Politics in Israel.* Boston: Little, Brown & Co., 1967.

Kimche, Jon, and Kimche, David. *A Clash of Destinies: The Arab-Jewish War and the Founding of the State of Israel.* New York: Praeger, 1960.

Lilienthal, Alfred M. *What Price Israel.* Chicago: Regnery, 1953.

Taylor, Alan R. *Prelude to Israel: An Analysis of Zionist Diplomacy, 1897–1947.* New York: Philosophical Library, 1959.

Williams, Laurence F. *The State of Israel.* London: Faber, 1957.

PERIODICALS

Baker, A. "Democracy vs. Democratic State: The Other Schism in Israeli Life." *Issues* 20(1966):6.

Galanter, Marc. "A Dissent on Brother Daniel: Report on Israeli Law of Return." *Commentary*, July 1963.

Himmelfarb, Milton. "How Many Israels? Discrimination against Afro-Asian Jews." *Commentary*, January 1964.

Korn, R. "Eshkol's Official Plan for Israel and the Diaspora." *Issues* 19(1965):13. Full text of plan appears in Israeli Government Year Book, 1965.

Roots, John McCook. "Peace Is More Important than Real Estate." *Saturday Review*, 3 April 1971. Interview with David Ben Gurion.

Weiner, Herbert. "Mission to Israel." *Commentary*, August 1963. Religious discrimination.

JEWS

Berger, Elmer. *Judaism or Jewish Nationalism: The Alternative to Zionism.* New York: Bookman Associates, 1957.

Dunlop, D. M. *The History of the Jewish Khazars.* Princeton: Princeton University Press, 1954. Origins of Russian Jews.

Stember, Charles H. et al. *Jews in the Mind of America.* New York: Basic Books, 1966.

JORDAN (See also JORDAN RIVER and PALESTINE)

Glubb, John B. *The Story of the Arab Legion.* London: Hodder & Stoughton, 1948.

Glubb, John B. *A Soldier with the Arabs.* New York: Harper, 1957.

Morris, James. *The Hashemite Kings.* New York: Pantheon, 1959.

Peake, Frederick G. *History of Jordan and Its Tribes.* Miami: University of Miami Press, 1958.

JORDAN RIVER

Arab Palestine Office. *Commentary on Water Development in the Jordan Valley.* Beirut: 1954.

Berber, Fritz. *Rivers in International Law*. London: Stevens, 1959.
Great Britain, Palestine Royal Commission. *Report*. Parliamentary Papers Cmd. 5479, 1937.
Hays, James B. *T.V.A. on the Jordan*. Washington: Public Affairs Press, 1948.
Macdonald, Sir Murdoch. *Report on the Proposed Extension of Irrigation in the Jordan River Valley*. London, 1954.
Smith, Herbert A. *Economic Uses of International Rivers*. London: King, 1931.
United Nations, *Integrated River Basin Development*. Document E/1066 (1956).
United Nations, *Legal Aspects of Hydro-Electric Development of Rivers and Lakes of Common Interest*. Document E/ECE/136.

PERIODICALS

Foda, Ezzeldine. "The Diversion of the Jordan River." *Al Ahram* (Cairo), 15 August 1961.
Ionides, Michael G. "The Disputed Waters of the Jordan!" *Middle East Journal*, vol. 7 (1953).
Kenworthy, William F. "Joint Development of International Waters." *American Journal of International Law*, July 1960.
"Report of the Arab Technical Committee." *Egyptian Economic and Political Review*, October 1955.

KUWAIT (See PERSIAN GULF STATES)

LEBANON

Agwani, Mohammed S., ed. *The Lebanese Crisis, 1958*. New York: Asia Publishing House, 1965.
Binder, Leonard, ed. *Politics in Lebanon*. New York: Wiley, 1966.
Hitti, Phillip K. *Lebanon in History: From the Earliest Times to the Present*. London: Macmillan, 1957.
Longrigg, Stephen H. *Syria and Lebanon Under French Mandate*. London: Oxford, 1958.
Polk, William R. *The Opening of South Lebanon*. Cambridge: Harvard University Press, 1963.
Salibi, Kamal S. *The Modern History of Lebanon*. New York: Praeger, 1965.

PERIODICALS

Entelis, J. P. "The Republic of Lebanon: A Political Development Analysis." *Arab Journal* 3(1966):47.
Garrett, Stephen C. "Lebanon's Race Against Time." *Progressive*, January 1970.
Hudson, M. C. "The Electoral Process and Political Development in Lebanon." *Middle East Journal* 20(1966):173.

LIBYA

Khadduri, Majid. *Modern Libya: A Study in Political Development.* Baltimore: Johns Hopkins Press, 1963.

Kubbah, Abdul Amir Q. *Libya: Its Oil Industry and Economic System.* Baghdad: Arab Petro-Economic Research Center, 1964.

Royal Institute of International Affairs. *Libya: A Brief Political and Economic Survey.* London: Oxford, 1957.

PERIODICALS

Winslow, R. S. "The New Libya: Where Even the Poor Can Dream." *National Observer,* 6 September 1965.

Zarrugh, M. Y. "The Petroleum Industry in Libya." *Arab Journal* 3(1966):13.

MOROCCO

Ashford, Douglas E. *Perspectives of a Moroccan Nationalist.* Englewood Cliffs, N.J.: Bedminster, 1964.

Cohen, Mark I., and Hahn, Lorna. *Morocco: Old Land, New Nation.* New York: Praeger, 1966.

Hoffman, Eleanor. *Realm of the Evening Star: A History of Morocco and the Lands of the Moors.* New York: Chilton, 1965.

Landau, Rom. *Morocco Independent Under Mohammed the Fifth.* London: Allen & Unwin, 1961.

Stewart, Charles F. *The Economy of Morocco, 1912–1962.* Cambridge: Harvard University Press, 1964.

PERIODICALS

Brownfeld, Allen C. "The Jews of Morocco." *Arab World,* September/October 1970.

Cooley, John K. "King Hassan's Unbound Morocco." *Reporter,* 11 October 1962.

Sterling, Claire. "Morocco's Troubled Young King." *Reporter,* 17 June 1965.

Wallenstein, Marcel. "The Moroccan Affair." *Chicago Tribune,* 26 March 1967. Mehdi ben Barka case.

NATIONALISM AND REVOLUTION (See also Individual Countries)

Al Razzaz, Munif. *The Evolution of the Meaning of Nationalism.* Toronto: Doubleday, 1963.

Antonius, George. *The Arab Awakening.* Toronto: Lippincott, 1939.

Eban, Abba. *The Tide of Nationalism.* New York: Horizon Press, 1959.

El Fassi, Allal. *The Independence Movements in Arab North Africa.* Washington: American Council of Learned Societies, 1954.

Haim, Sylvia G., ed. *Arab Nationalism: An Anthology.* Los Angeles: University of California Press, 1962.

Karpat, Kemal H., ed. *Political and Social Thought in the Contemporary Middle East.* New York: Praeger, 1968.

Nuseibeh, Hazem Z. *The Ideas of Arab Nationalism.* Ithaca: Cornell University Press, 1956.

Sayegh, Fayez A. *Arab Unity: Hope and Fulfillment.* New York: Devin-Adair, 1958.

Sharabi, Hisham B. *Nationalism and Revolution in the Arab World.* Princeton: Van Nostrand, 1966.

Zeine, Zeine N. *The Emergence of Arab Nationalism.* Beirut: Khayats, 1966.

PERIODICALS

Carmichael, Joel. "The Nature of Arab Nationalism." *Midstream,* Autumn, 1958.

Finer, Herman. "Reflections on the Nature of Arab Nationalism." *Middle Eastern Affairs,* October 1958.

Hourani, Albert H. "Near Eastern Nationalism Yesterday and Today." *Foreign Affairs,* December 1963.

Peretz, Don. "Arab Nationalism on the March." *Progressive,* November 1958.

Salem, Elie A. "Arab Nationalism: A Reappraisal." *International Affairs* (Canada), Summer 1962.

Sayegh, Fayez A. "Arab Nationalism and Soviet-American Relations." *Annals of the American Academy,* July 1959.

Williams, Keith, "The Meaning of Arab Nationalism." *Texas Quarterly,* Winter 1958.

OIL

Barrows, Gordon H. *The International Petroleum Industry.* New York: International Petroleum Institute, 1965.

Cattan, Henry. *The Evolution of Oil Concessions in the Middle East and North Africa.* Dobbs Ferry, N.Y.: Oceana, 1967.

Engler, Robert. *The Politics of Oil.* New York: Macmillan, 1961.

Finnie, David H. *Desert Enterprise: The Middle East Oil Industry in its Local Environment.* Cambridge: Harvard University Press, 1958.

Frankel, Paul H. *Oil: The Facts of Life.* London: Weidenfeld & Nicolson, 1962.

Hartshorn, J. E. *Oil Companies and Governments.* London: Faber, 1962.

Hirst, David. *Oil and Public Opinion in the Middle East.* London: Faber, 1966.

Issawi, Charles, and Yeganeh, Mohammed. *The Economics of Middle Eastern Oil.* New York: Praeger, 1963.

Leeman, Wayne A. *The Price of Middle East Oil*. Ithaca: Cornell University Press, 1962.

Lenczowski, George. *Oil and State in the Middle East*. Ithaca: Cornell University Press, 1960.

Longrigg, Stephen H. *Oil in the Middle East*. London: Oxford, 1967.

Mikdashi, Zuhayr. *A Financial Analysis of Middle Eastern Oil Concessions, 1901–1965*. New York: Praeger, 1966.

Mikesell, Raymond F., and Chenery, Hollis B. *Arabian Oil: America's Stake in the Middle East*. Chapel Hill: University of North Carolina Press, 1949.

Siksek, Simon G. *The Legal Framework for Oil Concessions in the Arab World*. Beirut: Middle East Research & Publishing Center, 1960.

Stocking, George W. *Middle East Oil*. Nashville: Vanderbilt University Press, 1970.

PERIODICALS

Hughes, Edward. "The Russians Drill Deep in the Middle East." *Fortune*, July 1968.

Margello, Clem. "Wall Street: Oil and the Mideast Crisis." *Newsweek*, 14 June 1967.

Scheer, Robert. "Oil and the Arabs." *Ramparts*, January 1968.

OMAN (See PERSIAN GULF STATES)

PALESTINE (See also BALFOUR DECLARATION and REFUGEES)

Bethmann, Erich W. *Decisive Years in Palestine: 1918–1948*. New York: American Friends of the Middle East, 1957.

Darwazah, al-Hakim. *A Short Survey of the Palestine Problem*. Beirut: Research Center, Palestine Liberation Organization, 1966.

Erskine, Beatrice. *Palestine of the Arabs*. London: George Harrap, 1935.

Granovsky, Abraham. [Granott, Abraham]. *The Land System in Palestine: History and Structure*. Trans. M. Simon. London: Eyre & Spottiswoode, 1952.

Hadawi, Sami, ed. *Palestine Partitioned, 1947–58*. New York: Arab Information Center, 1959.

Hadawi, Sami. *Palestine Before the United Nations*. Beirut: Institute for Palestine Studies, 1966.

Himadah, Sa'id, ed. *Economic Organization of Palestine*. Beirut: American Press, 1938.

Jeffries, Joseph M. N. *Palestine: The Reality*. London: Longmans Green, 1939.

Leonard, Leonard L. *The United Nations and Palestine*. New York: Carnegie Endowment for International Peace, 1949.

Loftus, P. J. *The National Income of Palestine, 1945*. Jerusalem, 1948.

Marlowe, John. *The Seat of Pilate*. London: Cresset, 1959.

Nathan, Robert R., Glass, Oscar, and Creamer, Daniel. *Palestine: Problem and Promise: An Economic Study*. Washington, D.C.: Public Affairs Press, 1946.

Palestine. Census Office. *Census of Palestine, 1931*. 2 vols. Alexandria, 1933.

————. *Report and General Abstracts of the Census of 1922* (taken 23rd October 1922). Comp. J. B. Barton. Jerusalem: Greek Convent Press, 1923.

————. Department of Migration. *The Statistics of Migration and Naturalization* [1934–]. Jerusalem, 1935–.

————. Office of Statistics. *Statistical Abstract for Palestine*, 1936–37– [1945–46]. Jerusalem: Government Printers Office, 1937–47.

————. *Vital Statistics Bulletin* (quarterly). Jerusalem: Office of Statistics, 1936–47.

Parkes, James W. *A History of Palestine from 135 A.D. to Modern Times*. New York: Oxford, 1949.

Polk, William R. et al. *Backdrop to Tragedy: The Struggle for Palestine*. Boston: Beacon, 1957.

Robnet, George W. *Conquest Through Immigration: How Zionism Turned Palestine into a Jewish State*. Pasadena, Calif.: Institute for Special Research, 1968.

Sharabi, Hisham B. *Palestine and Israel: The Lethal Dilemma*. New York: Pegasus, 1969.

PERIODICALS

Bassiouni, M. Cherif. "The Palestinians: Refugees or a People?" *Catholic World*, September 1970, pp. 257–62.

Childers, Erskine B. "Palestine: The Broken Triangle." *Journal of International Affairs*, (London) 19(1965):87–9.

Dorsey, William H., Jr. "Arab Commandos." *New Republic*, 22 November 1969, pp. 19–21.

Hunt, Ridgeley. "The Fedayeen: Fighters Without Friends." *Chicago Tribune Magazine*, 3 August 1969.

Toynbee, Arnold. "The Palestine Question." *Islamic Literature, April 1966*.

PALESTINE PRIOR TO 1917

De Haas, Jacob. *History of Palestine: The Last Two Thousand Years*. New York: Macmillan, 1934.

Great Britain. Foreign Office. Historical Section. Handbooks. *Syria and Palestine* [Handbook no. 60]. London: H.M.S.O., 1920.

Tibawi, Abdul Latif. *British Interests in Palestine, 1800–1901: A Study of Religious and Educational Enterprise*. London: Oxford University Press, 1961.

Wavell, Archibald P. *The Palestine Campaigns*. London: Constable, 1928.

Zeine, Zeine N. *The Struggle for Arab Independence: Western Diplomacy and the Rise and Fall of Faisal's Kingdom in Syria*. Beirut: Khayats, 1960.

PALESTINE: 1917–1948

Begin, Menahem W. *The Revolt: Story of the Irgun*. Trans. Samuel Katz. New York: Schuman, 1951.

Bernadotte af Wisborg, Folke. *To Jerusalem*. Trans. Joan Bulman. London: Hodder & Stoughton, 1951.

Cattan, Henry. *Palestine, The Arabs and Israel: The Search for Justice*. London: Longmans, 1969.

Edwardes, O. S. *Palestine: Land of Broken Promise: A Statement of the Facts Concerning Palestine and an Examination of the Anglo-American Commission*. London: Dorothy Crisp, 1946.

Esco Foundation for Palestine, Inc. *Palestine: A Study of Jewish, Arab and British Policies*. 2 vols. New Haven: Yale University Press, 1947.

Hurewitz, Jacob C. *The Struggle for Palestine*. New York: Norton, 1950.

Royal Institute of International Affairs. Information Department. *Great Britain and Palestine, 1915–1945*. 1937. Rev. ed. New York: Oxford University Press, 1946.

Sakran, Frank Charles. *Palestine Dilemma: Arab Rights Versus Zionist Aspirations*. Washington, D. C.: Public Affairs Press, 1948.

Sayegh, Fayez A. *Zionist Colonialism in Palestine*. Beirut: Research Center, Palestine Liberation Organization, 1965.

PERSIAN GULF STATES

Brinton, Jasper Y. *Aden and the Federation of South Arabia*. Washington: American Society of International Law, 1964.

Dickson, Harold R. P. *Kuwait and Her Neighbors*. London: Allen & Unwin, 1956.

Holden, David. *Farewell to Arabia*. New York: Walker & Co., 1966.

Johnston, Sir Charles. *The View from Steamer Point*. London: Collins, 1964.

Marlowe, John. *The Persian Gulf in the Twentieth Century*. New York: Praeger, 1962.

Phillips, Wendell. *Unknown Oman*. New York: McKay, 1966.

Wilson, Sir Arnold T. *The Persian Gulf: An Historical Sketch from the Earliest Times to the Beginning of the Twentieth Century*. London: Allen & Unwin, 1954.

PERIODICALS

Contini, Jeanne. "The Winds of Change in the Garden of Aden." *Reporter*, 4 July 1963, pp. 28–30.

Hollingsworth, Clare. "The Aden Dilemma." *Manchester Guardian Weekly*, 21 October 1965.

Morris, James. "Sundown at Aden." *Manchester Guardian Weekly*, 31 March 1966.

"Vest Pocket States of Arabia." *Newsweek*, 28 March 1966, p. 50.

Smith, Hedrick. "Britain's Little Vietnam." *New York Times*, 2 July 1967.

Thomas, Roy E. "The Persian Gulf Region." *Current History*, January 1971.

REFUGEES (See also PALESTINE and individual Arab countries)

Anderson, Per Olow. *They Are Human, Too*. Chicago: Regnery, 1957.

Rony, Gabbay. *A Political Study of the Arab-Jewish Conflict: The Arab Refugee Problem*. Geneva: Libraire Droz, 1959.

PERIODICALS

Brady, Thomas F. "Arab Refugees Long for Their Home." *New York Times*, 21 March 1966.

"Arab Refugee Problem Dynamite for Diplomats." *Christian Science Monitor*, 13 June 1957.

Eban, Abba. "Freedom With Knowledge." UNESCO Courier, 16(July 1963):10–13.

Gellhorn, Martha. "Why the Refugees Fled." *Manchester Guardian Weekly*, 3 August 1967.

Howard, Harry N. "UNRWA, the Arab Host Countries and the Refugees." *Middle East Forum*, 1966.

Manley, Chesley. "Arab Refugees Insist on Return to Palestine." *Chicago Tribune*, 18 January 1959.

Michelmore, Laurence. "UNRWA and the Palestine Refugees." *World Refugee Report*, 1966–67. Annual UN survey.

Syrkin, Marie "The Arab Refugees: A Zionist View." *Commentary*, January 1966, pp. 23–30.

SAUDI ARABIA

De Gaury, Gerald. *Faisal, King of Saudi Arabia*. London: Arthur Barker, 1966.

Howarth, David. *The Desert King*. New York: McGraw-Hill, 1964.

Philby, Harry St. J. *Saudi Arabia*. New York: Praeger, 1955.

PERIODICALS

Abercrombie, Thomas J. "Saudi Arabia: Beyond the Sands of Mecca." *National Geographic*, January 1966, pp. 1–53.

Rentz, George. "Saudi Arabia: Islamic Island." *Journal of International Affairs* 19, no. 1 (1965).

Sheean, Vincent. "King Faisal's First Year." *Foreign Affairs*, January 1966, pp. 304–13.

SOUTH YEMEN (See PERSIAN GULF STATES)

SOVIET UNION IN THE ARAB WORLD

Jansen, Godfrey H. *Nonalignment and the Afro-Asian States.* New York: Praeger, 1966.

Laqueur, Walter Z. *The Struggle for the Middle East: The Soviet Union and the Middle East, 1958–1968.* New York: Macmillan, 1969.

Tansky, Leo. *U.S. and U.S.S.R. Aid to Developing Countries.* New York: Praeger, 1969.

PERIODICALS

Gasteyger, Curt. "Moscow and the Mediterranean." *Foreign Affairs,* July 1968, pp. 676–87

Laqueur, Walter Z. "Russia Enters the Middle East." *Foreign Affairs,* June 1969.

Millar, T. B. "Soviet Policies South and East of Suez." *Foreign Affairs,* October 1970, pp. 70–80.

"Soviet Power in the Middle East." *Newsweek,* 17 February 1969.

"Moscow Fishes in Troubled Waters." *New York Times,* 3 December 1967.

Sayegh, Fayez A. "Arab Nationalism and Soviet-American Relations." *Annals of the American Academy,* July 1959.

Shwadran, Benjamin. "The Soviet Union in the Middle East." *Current History.* February 1967.

Tibawi, Abdul Latif. "Russian Cultural Penetration of Syria and Palestine in the Nineteenth Century." *Central Asian Journal* (London), October 1966.

SUDAN

Barbour, Kenneth M. *The Republic of the Sudan.* London: University of London, 1961.

Holt, Peter M. *A Modern History of the Sudan.* New York: Grove, 1961.

Oduho, Joseph, and Deng, William. *The Problem of the Southern Sudan.* New York: Oxford, 1963.

PERIODICALS

Shaffer, N. M. "The Sudan: Arab-African Confrontation." *Current History,* March 1966.

SUEZ CANAL

Bruchell, S. C., and Issawi, Charles. *Building the Suez Canal.* New York: American Heritage, 1966.

Eayrs, James, ed. *The Commonwealth and Suez: A Documentary Survey.* New York: Oxford, 1964.

Epstein, Leon D. *British Politics in the Suez Crisis.* Urbana: University of Illinois Press, 1964.

Finer, Herman. *Dulles Over Suez.* Chicago: Quadrangle Books, 1964.

Lauterpacht, E., ed. *The Suez Canal Settlement: A Selection of Documents, October 1956–March 1959.* New York: Praeger, 1960.

Marlowe, John. *World Ditch: The Making of the Suez Canal.* New York: Macmillan, 1964.

Nutting, Anthony. *No End of a Lesson: The Story of Suez.* New York: Potter, 1967.

Robertson, Terence. *Crisis: The Inside Story of the Suez Conspiracy.* New York: Atheneum, 1965.

Thomas, Hugh. *Suez.* New York: Harper, 1967.

U. S. Department of State. *The Suez Canal Problem, July 26–September 22, 1956.* Washington: Government Printing Office, 1956.

Watt, Donald C. *Britain and the Suez Canal.* London: Royal Institute of International Affairs, 1956.

PERIODICALS

Bassiouni, M. Cherif. "The Nationalization of the Suez Canal and the Illicit Act in International Law." *De Paul Law Review,* 4, no. 2(1965):258–98.

Dean, V. M. "Aswan and Suez." *Foreign Policy Bulletin,* 36(15 September 1956):6.

Epstein, Leon D., and Walker-Smith, Henderson. "Foreign Policy and Domestic Politics." *Political Science Quarterly,* September 1965.

Feis, Herbert. "Suez Scenario: A Lamentable Tale." *Foreign Affairs,* July 1960.

Malone, J. J. "Germany and the Suez Crisis." *Middle East Journal,* Winter 1966.

Marushkin, B. "Dulles's Suez Script." *International Affairs* (Moscow), 5 May 1963.

Mirsky, Georgy. "Suez in Retrospect." *New Times* (Moscow), 26 October 1966.

Smolansky, O. M. "Moscow and the Suez Crisis, 1956: A Reappraisal." *Political Science Quarterly,* December 1965, pp. 581–605.

SYRIA

Abu Jaber, Kamel S. *The Arab Ba'th Socialist Party: History, Ideology, and Organization.* Syracuse: Syracuse University Press, 1966.

Copeland, Paul W. *The Land and People of Syria.* Philadelphia: Lippincott, 1964.

Hitti, Philip K. *A History of Syria, including Lebanon and Palestine.* New York: Macmillan, 1957.

Longrigg, Stephen H. *Syria and Lebanon Under French Mandate.* London: Oxford, 1958.

Seale, Patrick. *The Struggle for Syria: A Study of Post-War Arab Politics, 1945-58.* New York: Oxford, 1965.

Torrey, Gordon H. *Syrian Politics and the Military, 1945–1958.* Columbus: Ohio State University Press, 1964.

Zuwiyya-Yamak, Labib. *The Syrian Social Nationalist Party: An Ideological Analysis.* Cambridge: Harvard University Press, 1966.

PERIODICALS

Comay, M. "Israel's Case Against Syria." *Midstream,* August/September 1966.

Palmer, Monte. "The United Arab Republic: An Assessment of Its Failure." *Middle East Journal,* Winter 1966, pp. 50–67.

Tibawi, Abdul Latif. "Russian Cultural Penetration of Syria and Palestine in the Nineteenth Century. *Central Asian Journal* (London), October 1966.

TUNISIA

Brace, Richard M. *Morocco, Algeria, Tunisia.* Englewood Cliffs: Prentice-Hall, 1964.

Laitman, Leon. *Tunisia Today.* New York: Citadel, 1954.

Micaud, Charles A. *Tunisia: The Politics of Modernization.* New York: Praeger, 1964.

Sabini, J.A.P. [John Anthony]. *Tunisia.* New York: Scribner, 1962.

Ziadeh, Nicola A. *Origins of Nationalism in Tunisia.* Beirut: Khayats, 1962.

PERIODICALS

Bourguiba, Habib. "The Tunisian Way." *Foreign Affairs,* April 1966, pp. 480–8.

Douqaji, J. "Some Aspects of the Economic Development of Tunisia." *Arab Journal,* no. 2 (1965/66).

Watt, Donald C. "Bourguiba, The Arabs and Palestine." *World Today,* June 1965, pp. 223–5.

UNITED STATES AND WESTERN POWERS IN THE ARAB WORLD

Abdul-Rahman, Asa'd. *United States and West German Aid to Israel: Facts and Figures.* Beirut: Palestine Liberation Organization, 1966.

Dowty, Allen. "Does the United States Have a Real Interest in Supporting Israel?" in *Great Issues of International Politics,* ed. Morton Kaplan. Chicago: Aldine, 1970.

Gallagher, Charles F. *The United States and North Africa.* Cambridge: Harvard University Press, 1963.

Hall, Harvey Porter. *American Interests in the Middle East.* New York: Foreign Policy Association, 1948.

Hirszowicz, Lukasz. *The Third Reich and the Arab East.* Toronto: University of Toronto Press, 1966.

Jansen, G. H. *Nonalignment and the Afro-Asian States.* New York: Praeger, 1966.

Polk, William R. *The United States and the Arab World.* Cambridge: Harvard University Press, 1969.

Safran, Nadav. *The United States and Israel.* Cambridge, Mass.: Harvard University Press, 1963.

Spielman, William C. *The United States in the Middle East.* New York: Pageant, 1959.

PERIODICALS

Badeau, John S. "U.S.A. and U.A.R.: A Crisis in Confidence." *Foreign Affairs*, January 1965, pp. 281–96.

Bitar, E. "Toward Better Arab-American Understanding." *Arab Journal*, 3(1966):40.

Bustani, Emil. "The Arab World and Britain." *International Journal* (London), October 1959.

Campbell, John C. "The Arab-Israeli Conflict: An American Policy." *Foreign Affairs*, October 1970, pp. 51–69.

Glubb, John B. "Britain and the Arabs." *Central Asian Journal*, July, October 1969.

Hartley, Anthony. "The United States, the Arabs, and Israel." *Commentary*, March 1970, pp. 45–50.

Hurewitz, Jacob C. "Our Mistake in the Middle East." *Atlantic*, December 1956, pp. 46–52.

Issawi, Charles. "Negotiation from Strength? A Reappraisal of Western-Arab Relations." *International Affairs*, January 1959, pp. 102–12.

Kenen, J. L. "American Policy in the Middle East." *Jewish Frontier*, December 1963.

Mates, Leo. "Nonalignment and the Great Powers." *Foreign Affairs*, April 1970, pp. 525–36.

Nolte, Richard H. "Arab Nationalism and the Cold War." *Yale Review*, September 1959, pp. 1–19.

WAR OF 1967

Bar-On, Mordechai, ed. *Israel Defense Forces: The Six-Day War.* Philadelphia: Chilton, 1968.

Bashan, Raphael. *The Victory: The Six-Day War of 1967.* Ed. O. Zmora, Chicago: Quadrangle, 1968.

Blaxland, Gregory. *Egypt and Sinai: Eternal Battle Ground.* New York: Funk and Wagnalls, 1968.

Byford-Jones, W. *The Lightning War: The Israeli-Arab Conflict*. Indianapolis: Bobbs-Merrill, 1968.

Cattan, Henry. *Palestine, the Arabs and Israel*. London: Longmans, Green, 1969.

Chace, James, ed. *Conflict in the Middle East*. New York: H. W. Wilson Co., 1968.

Churchill, Randolph S., and Churchill, Winston S. *The Six-Day War*. Boston: Houghton Mifflin, 1967.

Dodd, Peter, and Barakat, Halim. *River Without Bridges: A Study of the Exodus of the 1967 Palestinian Arab Refugees*. Beirut: Institute for Palestine Studies, 1968.

Douglas-Home, Charles. *The Arabs and Israel*. London: Bodley Head, 1968.

Draper, Theodore. *Israel and World Politics: Roots of the Third Arab-Israeli War*. New York: Viking, 1968.

Gervasi, Frank. *The Case for Israel*. New York: Viking, 1967.

Glubb, Sir John B. *The Middle East Crisis: A Personal Interpretation*. London: Hodder and Stoughton, 1967.

Hadawi, Sami. *The Arab-Israeli Conflict (Cause and Effect)*. Beirut: Institute for Palestine Studies, 1967.

———. *Bitter Harvest: Palestine Between 1914–1967*. New York: New World Press, 1967.

———. *Palestine in Focus*. Beirut: Institute for Palestine Studies, 1968.

Halderman, John W., ed. *The Middle East Crisis: Test of International Law*. Special issue of *Law and Contemporary Problems*, 23 (Winter, 1968).

Higgins, Rosalyn. *United Nations Peacekeeping, 1946–1967: Documents and Commentary*. The Middle East, vol. 1. New York: Oxford, 1969.

Keesing's Research Report. *The Arab-Israeli Conflict: The 1967 Campaign*. New York: Scribner, 1968.

Kerr, Malcolm H. *The Middle East Conflict*. Headline Series, no. 191. New York: Foreign Policy Association, 1968.

Khadduri, Majdia, ed. *The Arab-Israeli Impasse: Expressions of Moderate Viewpoints on the Arab-Israeli Conflict by Well-Known Western Writers*. Washington: Robert D. Luce, 1969.

Kimche, David, and Bawley, Dan. *The Sandstorm: The Arab-Israeli War of June, 1967: Prelude and Aftermath*. New York: Stein and Day, 1968.

Kishon, Ephraim, and Dosh, K. *So Sorry We Won*. New York: Bloch, 1968.

Kosut, Hal, ed. *Israel and the Arabs: The June 1967 War*. New York: Facts on File, Interim History, 1968.

Lall, Arthur. *The UN and the Middle-East Crisis, 1967*. New York: Columbia University Press, 1968.

Laqueur, Walter Z. *The Road to Jerusalem: The Origins of the Arab-Israeli Conflict, 1967*. New York: Macmillan, 1968.

Love, Kenneth. *Suez: The Twice-Fought War*. New York: McGraw-Hill, 1969.

Marshall, S. L. A. *Swift Sword: The Historical Record of Israel's Victory, June, 1967*. New York: American Heritage. 1967.

Resistance of the West Bank Arabs to Israeli Occupation. New York: New World Press, 1967.

Safran, Nadav. *From War to War: The Arab-Israeli Confrontation, 1948-1967*. New York: Pegasus, 1969.

Vance, Vick, and Laver, Pierre. *Hussein of Jordan: My War with Israel*. New York : William Morrow, 1969.

PERIODICALS AND DOCUMENTS

Abu-Lughod, Ibrahim. "The Arab-Israeli Confrontation: Some Thoughts on the Future." *Arab Journal*, 5(1968):13–23.

Bassiouni, M. Cherif. "The Middle East in Transition: From War to War, A Proposed Solution." *The International Lawyer*, 4(1970): 379.

Deutscher, Isaac. "On the Arab-Israeli War." *Arab Journal*, 5(Summer, 1968):36. Reprinted from *New Left Review*, July–August, 1967, pp. 30–45.

Horton, Alan W. "The Arab-Israeli Conflict of June 1967: Part I: Some Immediate Issues." AUFS Reports Service: Northeast Africa Series, vol. 13, no. 2. New York: American Universities Field Staff, 1967.

Howard, Michael, and Hunter, Robert. *Israel and the Arab World: The Crisis of 1967*. Adelphi Papers, no. 41. London: Institute for Strategic Studies, October, 1967.

"The Israeli-Arab War and the Future Socialism." *International Socialist Journal*, August, 1967, p. 513.

"Oil and Arabs." *Ramparts*, January, 1968, pp. 37–42.

Palestine War 1967. New York: New World Press, 1967.

Peretz, Martin. "The American Left and Israel." *Commentary*, November, 1967, pp. 27–34.

Reynar, Anthony S. "The Straits of Tiran and the Sovereignty of the Sea." *Middle East Journal*, 21 (1967):404.

Stone, I. F. "Holy War." *New York Review of Books*, 3 August 1967.

"The Story of Two Wars." *Ramparts*, November, 1967, pp. 85–98.

Yost, Charles. "The Arab-Israeli War: How It Began." *Foreign Affairs*, 46(1968):304–20.

YEMEN

Bethmann, Erich W. *Yemen on the Threshold*. Washington: American Friends of the Middle East, 1960.

Helfritz, Hans. *Yemen: A Secret Journey*. London: Allen & Unwin, 1958.

Ingrams, William H. *The Yemen: Imams, Rulers and Revolutions*, New York: Praeger, 1964.

PERIODICALS

Edmund, Frank. "Starting from Scratch in the Yemen." *Manchester Guardian Weekly*, 13 August 1966.

ZIONISM (See also BALFOUR DECLARATION, JEWS, and ISRAEL)

Avnery, Uri. *Israel Without Zionists*. New York: Macmillan, 1968.

Basheer, Tahseen, ed. *Edwin Montagu and the Balfour Declaration*. New York: Arab League Office, 1966.

Batal, James. *Zionist Influence on the American Press*. Beirut: Nasser Press, 1956.

Ben-Gurion, David. *Israel: Years of Challenge*. New York: Holt, Rinehart & Winston, 1963.

———. *Rebirth and Destiny of Israel*. Trans. Mordekhai Nurock. New York: Philosophical Library, 1954.

Berger, Elmer. *The Jewish Dilemma*. New York: Devin-Adair, 1945.

———. . . . *Who Knows Better Must Say So!* New York: American Council for Judaism, 1955.

Buber, Martin. *Israel and the World: Essays in a Time of Crisis*. 2d ed. New York: Schocken Books, 1963.

Cohen, Israel. *A Short History of Zionism*. London: Frederick Muller, 1951.

———. *The Zionist Movement*. London: Frederick Muller, 1945.

Cooke, Hedley V. *Israel: A Blessing and a Curse*. London: Stevens, 1960.

Eban, Abba. *Voice of Israel*. New York: Horizon Press, 1957.

Goldmann, Nahum. *The Genius of Herzl and Zionism Today*. Jerusalem: Zionist Executive, 1955.

Halperin, Samuel. *The Political World of American Zionism*. Detroit: Wayne State University Press, 1961.

Halpern, Ben. *The Idea of the Jewish State*. Cambridge: Harvard University Press, 1961.

Hecht, Ben. *Perfidy*. New York: Julian Messner, 1962.

Hertzberg, Arthur, ed. *The Zionist Idea: A Historical Analysis and Reader*. 1959. New York: Atheneum, 1969.

Herzl, Theodor. *Complete Diaries*. Ed. Raphael Patai. Trans. Harry Zohn. 5 vols. New York: Herzl Press, 1960.

———. *Diaries*. Ed. and trans. Marvin Lowenthal. New York: Dial Press, 1956.